UNINTERRUPTED POETRY

PAUL ELUARD

UNINTERRUPTED POETRY:

Selected Writings

WITH ENGLISH TRANSLATIONS
BY LLOYD ALEXANDER
AND INTRODUCTORY NOTES BY
ARAGON, LOUIS PARROT
AND CLAUDE ROY

GALWAY COUNTY LIBRARIES

GREENWOOD PRESS, PUBLISHERS
WESTPORT, CONNECTICUT

Library of Congress Cataloging in Publication Data
Éluard, Paul, 1895-1952.
  Uninterrupted poetry.

    Published in 1951 under title: Selected writings.
    English and French.
    Reprint of the 1975 ed. published by New
  Directions Pub. Corp., New York.
    Bibliography: p.
    I. Alexander, Lloyd. II. Title.
  [PQ2609.L75A6 1977]   841'.9'12   77-22122
  ISBN 0-8371-9779-1

This edition originally published in 1975 by New Directions
Publishing Corporation.

Reprinted with the permission of New Directions Publishing Corporation.

Reprinted in 1977 by Greenwood Press,
A division of Congressional Information Service, Inc.
88 Post Road West, Westport, Connecticut 06881

Library of Congress catalog card number 77-22122
ISBN 0-8371-9779-1

Printed in the United States of America

10 9 8 7 6 5 4 3 2

C O N T E N T S

> *The poems are presented as nearly as possible
> in chronological order.   The dates at the top
> of each page indicate the year when the poem
> was first published in one of Eluard's books.*

PAUL ELUARD

H E is large, with a large body, a large forehead, a large nose; but he has a way of being large that is heavy, seated, square, and massive. Eluard is large with lightness, much too attentive to be called as large as a cloud (the case with Supervielle, for example), infinitely too *present*, a man of flesh, hair, bones, hands, looks, to be called large as a large cloud of smoke. But he is extremely light. He has a fairly grave voice; he articulates very well, gesturing while speaking words gently and ceremoniously; reciting verses very well, his own and those of others. He expresses poetry as it should be : with a singing simplicity. The records he has made commercially or for the radio are very fine. His face could be inscribed in a long rectangle. A handsome face, well covered with flesh, with years, with thoughts and *good* sentiments. Rather sanguine, although the word evokes a way of being which is not at all Eluard, who knows, however, how to turn quite pink after a good dinner — a thing he does not despise. What we must say is that Eluard is a man irrigated with blood. Which is not evident in everyone : there are people we say have electricity in their veins (like Aragon), or snow (like Maurice Blanchot), or wind (like many others). Above greying eyebrows he has a fine space of forehead up to his hair which is brushed straight back, neither too long nor too short.

Eluard is always very elegant, well-groomed, and he wears hats. He smokes enormously (too much). Even though his hands tremble a little and he is too demanding on his health, even in anger, or dogged by events, or baited (he has been, a little) he has a type of slow majesty that is very remarkable. It is not at all the stiff, withdrawing, artificial majesty of someone who hoists himself up, stretches himself out, and raises his collar (and tone) to make an impression. Eluard has the easy majesty natural to the truly great of this world : Targui chieftains, racehorses, children at play, certain fish, and grey-pink gladiole.

With him, even the most weighty things have this majestic lightness, a little childlike. Since long before the war, Eluard has been suffering with those who suffer, nourishing his rage against the persecutors, his hate against the wicked and the stupid, and his tenderness for the innocent. I saw him grow pale, pale, pale in the Rue de Dragon one morning in 1944, while waiting for the cyclist from a clandestine printer who did not always come. He did everything : action against the Germans, dangerous things or simply boring things; envelopes to glue shut, tracts to fold; a minute and disconcerting way to pass the time. Living with him, one completely forgot that poets *too* can be assassinated : Lorca, Saint-Pol Roux, Max Jacob, Desnos. For example, Eluard had to hide, find a refuge. For other clandestine workers that would have meant a small valise, a toothbrush in a pocket, or nothing more than taking a run-out powder. But Eluard did not move without his universe. In his apartment-hiding-place he brought with him, minutely, all he needed to live : Nusch his wife, of course; and he had no money, no papers (unless false), no address, but walls covered with Picasso,

Miro, Max Ernst, Leger, original editions which he has such a pleasant way of caressing with his fingertips. Then, when he had nothing more to eat, he sold a little package of fine books. Since then, of course, there are people who smile, who insinuate that all that wasn't really serious; but for myself at that time (a little frightened), I could never succeed in getting this idea out of my head : that if Paul Eluard the poet had been arrested by the Gestapo, perhaps tragic things would have happened to Paul Eluard of the Resistance. He never dreamed of them. There was, in this black and groping epoch, a bizarre parenthesis in Paul Eluard's life: the few months he spent at Saint-Alban, a sanatorium for the insane. Louis Parrot has told this story admirably.

He is fifty. He was born in the suburbs, in Saint-Denis where there is a basilica of kings and the factory smokestacks of the proletariat. He has travelled widely. Rather than say that he has seen many countries, we should say that many countries have seen him, have had the surprise and honor to see Paul Eluard. One day he departed without leaving any address (to make a tour of the world). He has been sick in Switzerland, gassed in the war, in good health at Cornouailles, happy in Spain or Italy. He has been in both wars; the first in the trenches, the second at the railroad front (in 1939), then afterwards at the front of the Resistance. He lives on the Rue de la Chapelle (*now Rue Marx-Dormoy — Ed.*), a grey, cobbled neighborhood, noisy and unassuming. In a working-class house, with no red-carpeted stairs, Eluard has a little honeycomb cell, three narrow, well-arranged rooms with everything you could ask for in the way of fine books, beautiful paintings, and *objets d'art :* pre-Columbian statuettes, a king on a throne sculptured by a madman, Chagalls, Chiricos, Massons, Picassos, Dalis: the only manuscript (in the world) of Isidore Ducasse, Comte de Lautréamont, a bronze death's-head, bound books, a hummingbird, an Easter Island statue, a chalk fetish from New Mecklemburg, a bust of Baudelaire : all that in a milieu of proper little curtains of blue oilcloth, like those on which we set cups of café-au-lait.

Eluard always has an air of availability, of sovereignty, but he is constantly traversed by loads of people; his friends first of all, and he believes in friendship, he needs friendship as he needs air, bread, books, the sky, and all the people of whom he thinks all the time, the ones who are sick, the ones who are unhappy, the ones whom men or life have wronged. He seems to live only on love and cold water and poetry, and a little whisky when there is any, but he lives the life of millions of men, he is a door, swinging open to all who are against injustice, to the Secretary of the Committee for the fight against this, the delegate from the Committee for the defense against that; his days are devoured by nice people with whom he is incredibly nice, by impatient people with whom he is extraordinarily patient. One doesn't know how to reconcile that with another aspect of Paul Eluard. This Paul Eluard who is the transparency of a dream, the inlaid clarity of a pure vision. Paul Eluard who is poetry made man. Poetry made man and woman, because Eluard has been not only Paul, but Nusch Eluard* who was tiny, slender, and gracious beside him, unbound and transparent as, as...? As the poetry of Paul Eluard. See all his love poems to find out what this shadow in his shadow is.

* With great sorrow we learned of her death in 1946. — Tr.

X

2

A being is interesting by his contradictions and defines himself by the response he gives them. I am looking for those of Paul Eluard, in his presence as a man and in his poet's voice. In his everyday life and attitude there is this mixture of secret man and public man, of lover and agitator, of the inward look and Revolution. And his poet's voice ? What is the voice of Eluard like, his way of writing? His poetry?

To whom does the poet Paul Eluard speak? We see very clearly to whom certain poets speak: that Musset addresses by turns his black-dressed double and the pit of the future Comédie-Française, that Nerval speaks to the night and Hugo to family-circle History, to Humanity, or to the first-form, Verlaine to Almighty God or a girl — or boy-friend, and Baudelaire to the most secret thing in all of us; Jules Romains to the subscribers of the Odeon's Thursdays. To whom does Eluard speak ? Well, first Eluard speaks to the present; Eluard invokes, evokes, makes the present instant familiar when the instant is that of a present, a gift. I ask that we see a little more than a play on words (frivolous) in this remark. What is most constant, most obsessing (most monotonous) in Eluard's poetry is the attempt to make it fix with words a certain privileged vision offered from time to time to the poet. « Man, » says Valéry, « possesses a certain look which makes him disappear; himself and all the rest, beings, earth, and sky; and which fixes itself in time out of time. » Perhaps it is not absolutely exact to say that the poem serves to fix this instant offered to the spirit by itself, for it may also serve, by evoking it, to reproduce it. To reconstitute it, to restore it artificially. A poem is a sensitive machinery of words conceived to make man other than what he is, a recipe for metamorphoses. For Eluard, it is a question of giving *back* to us, or *giving* us to see this image of a man marvelously happy, simplified, penetrating, penetrated; this instant when, as he says in *Shared Nights,* « there is no show. Remember, for solitude, the empty stage, without scenery, without actors, without musicians. They say: the theatre of the world, the world stage and we two, we no longer know what it is... Each one a shadow, but in the shadow we forget it. » There is no show, says Eluard; the beings, earth, and sky disappeared, says Valéry. The poet undertakes precisely to organize a spectacle of non-spectacle, and with the help of the words designating beings, earth, and sky, to express their absence, their absorption; it is a *senseless* undertaking. Eluard's poetry seems, in fact, very often not to have any direction, so contracted with enigma that it eludes the grasp and exerts none at all. It glides, steals away, and the slag of the work seems to efface itself, to dissolve of itself, leaving to subsist only these diamond *graffiti,* victories. Poems. To whom does Eluard speak ? In a low voice, to himself, to this accomplice of the shadow, this beloved woman who each day helps him reconquer this look which does not look, this absent presence, this evident, unspeakable magic which is his only reason (or fashion) for living.

Eluard's poetry always speaks to the ear, very close to the ear :

> *Here are the voices which no longer know what*
> *   they keep silent*
> *And here I speak*
> *Deafened yet hearing what I say*
> *And hearing myself I teach*

Is it very necessary to develop the comparisons imposed between this lyricism of the ineffable and the verses of mystics, Christian or otherwise? In order to hold to a tenacious *description* of this poetry, how can we avoid finding in it the constant traits of mystic poems, the extreme allusiveness, the breaking of the logical bonds and the refusal of transition; and this destruction of words one by the other, of the substantive by the epithet, the epithet by another epithet. Reading Eluard, one thinks constantly of the « éclatantes ténèbres » and the « nuits lumineuses » of Saint John of the Cross, of Angelus Silesius, or the Christian poets perpetuated by Abbé Bremond in his *Histoire du Sentiment Religieux.* Here expression is armed against itself, the phrase scarcely set down turns on itself to bite and wipe out its beginning.

A flight a return nothing had gone
All led to torment
All led to rest

says one poem. And this other, an expression of a perfect abandon of the spirit for which the mystics of Christianity or the Orient would offer so many equivalents : « Will is no longer the mask we remove, nor the eyes which open. She asks me neither to abdicate nor to hold. I am delivered, truly delivered, to the reality of a mirror which does not reflect my appearance... Without yesterday or tomorrow. This pure face begins again. »

It seems that Eluard, having attained these *spiritual* riverbanks, can never more turn back from them. One whole part of his work, the largest, seems to put it forever out of range of that which presses, pushes, destroys most humans. He is saved — or lost. Intensely absent, in any

XIII

case. Even if the spirit no longer spontaneously finds the mysterious effusion which tore it wordlessly away from itself, this grace and this present are *imitable*. A certain technique can reconquer them. Love, poetry, artificial paradises offer their assistance like a hazel wand to the sorcerer. Eluard has the miracle within reach of his hand, this hand which caresses a body, holds a pen, grips a glass. He can return at will to this space whose limits he overflows, to this state of man in which man destroys appearances, time, death, weight, thickness, sorrow, anguish.

It is precisely here that we await the Secretaries of the Committees for the defense of this and that who set up headquarters in Eluard's study, it is here that we await the poems of circumstance of Eluard. Here is the point of this vital contradiction which gives Eluard's existence such a pressing, vivacious, and obsessing interest. Such a necessary interest. This is what prevents going in circles. It's very unhealthy, going in circles. Very dangerous.

3

Paul Eluard offers us the example of a happy man to whom his happiness does not suffice — of a poet blessed with gifts and who does not satisfy himself with them. He can quit the universe when it pleases him; this universe is not always beautiful, and yet he stays. Men are not always good; he can escape them and refuses to do it. He, the freest of men, accepts himself as the most responsible. He takes as much care organizing fetters for himself as arranging his escapes. He has the power to surmount time and is passionately determined to live in this century. He knows how to be peaceful, but gives himself over, heart and fists bound to anger, despair or hate. « I have the power to exist without destiny », he says. And he forges himself a destiny, patiently, a man's destiny, tied to and sunk into the destiny of other men.

It is because he wants to *share* his discovery. He sees unhappiness, he feels for the unhappy, he guesses the tears flowing down cheeks in the darkness:

Tears of eyes unhappiness of the unhappy
Unhappiness without interest and tears without color

And he knows that man can be without tears and without unhappiness. He knows for he has been so. He knows because he has proven so. Another need, as alive and pressing as that of his own welfare leaves its mark: that of sharing:

All eyes face each other and equal glances
Share the wonder of being outside of time

There are many minds to think that man can only be the way he is, once and for all; that man is given, eternal, unchanging and unchangeable, that there is nothing new under the sun, especially not man; that the man of caverns and the métro, the man of Passy and the man of La Chapelle, the Negro and the steelworker, after all, are the same man and we'll get nothing more out of him, even by taming him, even by beating him. Man is a bizarre sort of object; there are ways of using him and not much for him to use; we must take him as he is, there are laws of human nature just as there are laws of nature not human, no need to knock your head against a wall, all we can hope is that by knocking the heads of those whose heads are less well-made, we may have a little peace; we'll stay among the right sort of people, in good company. There are many people to think that, to make themselves a reason and call it Reason, pronouncing it RRReason, and to discover reasonably that man is not reasonable and that there is no reason to think he can ever become so. They do not consider that at all hopeless; after all, what do you expect, men are men, it will always be six of one and half-a-dozen of the other, you can take them any which way since the beginning of time and there's no way out of it. There is a whole tribe of minds like that, they see no possible way out, they have nothing but sarcasm for the dreamers, cloud-riders, dream cavaliers, not-realists, poets, and madmen. That's that: man, a period; that's all. One final period. Man is that type of fairly constant pulp on which one can, if necessary, build up fine, rigid systems. Men are always the same because people say so.

But other people know *experimentally* that this is not true. The man who has been to war knows very well that tribulations reveal all sorts of surprisingly possible men among these living beings with sleeping appearances. The psychiatrist knows well that man contains a thousand sorts of follies beyond his wise reason. The traveller knows well that there are human verities for each side of the Pyrenees and of all mountains. And the poet knows well, he first, that man is extremely *possible,* in spite of those who insist on raising up, as Eluard says so magnificently:

The solemn geography of human limits.

Because Eluard himself *cannot* believe in a man with a plaster prototype like the detachable figures in medical supply stores, in a man hard-

ened, given, unmakeable. He has the concrete
experience of all the resources of the human
mind, of all the forms man can take. Of all the
chances for happiness there are in man (not the
happiness of an « epoch when the meaning of the
word happiness is degraded day by day until it
becomes a synonym for unconsciousness. ») There
is another humanity possible, another way of
being. « What is now proven was before only
imagined, » says Blake. It will be the task of the
poet to help men prove the truth of what he has
inspired, to help in the building of a different
world:

We shall all board a new memory
Together we shall speak a sensitive language

What the poet needs in order to feel himself
totally delivered, justified in his own welfare by
the welfare of all men, is the sharing of his
existence: « Poetry will make itself flesh and
blood only starting from the moment when it will
be reciprocal. This reciprocity is entirely a
function of the equality of happiness among
men. » Is it possible? Is it possible

That man delivered from his absurd past
Raises before his brother a like face
And gives vagabond wings to reason

It is possible, at least no one has ever tried it.
But it is not a personal adventure, a solitary
experience. It is not a question of every man for
himself and the devil take the hindmost. The
poet has seen himself *different* and has felt
himself saved, but it is stronger than he is, he
does not wish to be saved all alone. He cannot
be saved all alone.

XVII

But at this precise point a temptation is offered the poet as to all men of « good will, » and more strongly to the poet since he is a man of language and skilled in the bewitching, magical usage of language. It would seem quite natural that by *showing* a reasonable way to men that they will directly take to it, that by defining the condition of their metamorphosis they will directly bend to it, that by *speaking* to them one will succeed in reaching, them, fashioning them, changing them. Isn't it easy to awaken all the happy possibilities of man by speaking to him with force or eloquence, with persuasion or with knowledge? There are poets and writers who are revolted by the misery of this idiotic world, boisterous and blind. They want desperately to cry out to the people that there is a way to leave it, and they know that they have means so able, so subtle, and so efficacious of crying out that no one will be able to resist their call. This seems to me, for example, the attitude of that other friend of Paul Eluard, André Breton. Breton sees no way of rebirth for men other than docility to the predications of poets. He believes very strongly in the virtue of speeches: « It is a question of making recognizable, at any price, the artificial character of old antinomies... » he says. « The time has come to make worth-while the ideas of..., » he says. Make recognizable, he says. Make worth-while, he says. Only man is very odd, fertile in singular duplicities, very capable, for example, of recognizing and accepting a truth and then acting in a different direction. Men are curiously organized and, as Freud says (with melancholy), « Arguments can do nothing against their passions », and the truth which runs through what Marx magnificently names the « idealist entrails » of man goes

XVIII

to lose itself in the deserts of inefficacy, blotted out forever.

In 1942, Paul Eluard rejoined the foremost party of the French Resistance. « At a time when it was not easy, » he says. In order to be with those for whom killing Germans was not merely killing Germans but also helping man give birth to the best in him. In order to be with the handful of men who, to change the destiny of men, did not blame their « idealist entrails » but the world in which they were born, grew up and lived. A decisive act, surging up from a man who has explored, better than anyone else, the great inner expanses of the spirit, who has had *spiritual* adventures much more authentic than those of the defenders of a patent spiritualism, than those of the bragging annihilators of « degrading materialism, » than those of the characters with their hearts in their pure hands and their occidental eyes drenched with idealist tears who denounce the primacy of social values and the pagan cult of economy:

> *Beautiful evaporated birds*
> *They dream of their thoughts*
> *They weave themselves hats*
> *A hundred times larger than their heads*
> *They meditate their absence*
> *And hide in their own shadow.*

4

This is a rather sketchy Eluard I have just drawn, terribly linear. But I do not believe I have betrayed, essentially, the features of face and mind which I have chosen. I have only forgotten the most important. The most serious. Paul Eluard is a good man. Almost no one in our time is really good, goodness is a depreciated virtue, a little silly, a little old-fashioned, not in style or literature; and quite evidently Malraux is not *good,* nor Gide, nor Motherlant, nor Mauriac, nor Henri Michaux, nor Claudel, nor Aragon; and of course they laugh at it. But Eluard is good and he makes those about him relax, grow gentle and benevolent. He puts confidence in everyone, and almost every time he wins this bet: that men are good. For the ones who make him lose, for the real wicked, he has a hatred which is simple, frank, and entire; a beautiful hatred. A very good-quality hatred, without snarling, without calculation, which is that of the *good.*

Such is Paul Eluard.

Claude Roy.

XX

THE POET
AND THE WAR

I<small>N</small> his notes published at the end of *Au Rendez-
vous Allemand* which reprints several of his
best-known poems, Paul Eluard gives us further
clarification of the circumstances in which most
of them were written. Thus, the poems and the
commentaries that enrich them are doubly
precious to us. They explain each other recipro-
cally. The commentaries keep alive in us the
memory of the times which saw these poems'
birth, and links us to them by a thousand visible
bonds. The poems inform us, better than any
long chronicle, of the mental state of French intellectuals during the four occupation years. And if
these short passages, written with a moving simplicity, were not as perfect as the best prose pages
of Paul Eluard, they would still have the irrepla-
ceable value of fixing for us the oft-disputed
relationship between a poetic work and the times
which inspired it. How many poems has Eluard
taken from some banal epiode, some small fact
which would have furnished others with only
poor substance for a newspaper article. They
are still the same words, the same events of our
day; but the poet has given them their true
significance; he makes them live, regroups them
according to an order to which he has submitted
himself, without knowing the laws of it too well.

Thanks to him, the history of these past years, marked by so many incidents, happy and sad, hours of defeat or hope, passes in its entirety in a few verses which will preserve for us its image faithfully inscribed in a poetic memory that forgets nothing.

As a matter of fact, all who gave to the Resistance in the fullest measure of their means cannot forget the large part played by Paul Eluard in its organization. This poet, whom nothing seemingly designated to lead difficult and dangerous action, gave himself to it completely; at the same time that he was writing poems whose publication contributed immeasurably to the spiritual resurrection of France, he helped in rallying a great number of young writers.

My original critique*, first published in April, 1944, which tried to give a complete picture of the author of *Capitale de la Douleur,* was obliged to leave this activity in shadow; or at most only to forebode it. It did show, however, that there was no break in this work devoted entirely to Poetry, that is to say to truth, whose latest poems were the echo of the first known verses of Eluard, *Poèmes pour la Paix,* which appeared during the first World War. From that, the reader could easily guess the civic attitude adopted by their author during the four years of occupation.

« The pallid pre-war, the grey war of oppression with its eternal wonders » — later, during the winter of 1940-41 when he « remained, because of the cold, a month without opening the shutters. » to the epoch when « notices, threats, lists of hostages spread over the walls of Paris, striking fear

---

* Referring to *Paul Eluard,* a volume reprinted in the series *Poètes d'Aujourd'hui* (Editions Pierre Seghers) to which the above pages form an introduction. — Tr.

in some and shame in all » inspired some of Eluard's most celebrated poems. In them he sings the misery of a country which will not despair and which finds in its suffering the very reason for its revolt. He evokes Paris, Paris which sings no longer in the streets, her unresigned people, the faces of the innocent being led to death, the struggle carried on by so many heroes who had nothing left but the desire to wipe out the despicable invader. All who have met Paul Eluard in the streets of this city where he has always lived have understood the esteem in which he holds this people who « tolerate no injustice. » He went from one neighborhood to the other, carrying a brief-case loaded with forbidden papers and clandestine editions, each day risking recognition and arrest. After the publication of *Poésie et Vérité* 1942, which the German Institute denounced as a dangerous tract, he changed residence each month, taking with him only crumpled bits of paper on which he wrote the first drafts of his poems. For a long while his existence was one which so many intellectuals have known; but few of them have expressed, as he has, all its misery and grandeur.

Some of his poems — *Les Armes de la Douleur* in particular — are only poetic transcriptions of the sorrowful miscellany that the German newspapers in Paris and Vichy published each day in their chronicle of terrorism. Inspired by the events themselves, these admirable poems of circumstance were to make a redoubtable propaganda weapon in the hands of our partisans. They were published everywhere in France, multigraphed, reproduced in tracts circulating from one maquis to another. Eluard's poetic activity, which from that time on was to mix with his patriotic activity, multiplied. With Jean Lescure, he undertook the

XXIII

publication of *Honneur des Poètes* and *Europe,* collections of poems to which most of our poets of today contributed. We can judge the difficulties entailed in such a work. He had to gather texts, slip from under the surveillance of the Gestapo, and work daily with printers, typesetters, carriers, and all the people we never mention but to whom clandestine literature owes so much recognition. Later, we are again indebted to him for the initiative in preparing the *Almanach des Lettres Françaises,* finally produced by Georges Adam and Claude Morgan, principal animators of *Lettres Françaises.* Eluard helped edit this clandestine paper in which he published a long article on Max Jacob. A little while before the Liberation, when the dangers of publication had grown even greater, he completed the Péguy-Péri tract for *Les Editions de Minuit.* Whenever the Resistance needed help in making its voice heard, Eluard was present; this poet revealed himself as a man of action, courageous and lucid.

We remember the welcome given *Poésie et Vérité* 1942 by all free men. In *Une Seule Pensée* (I was born to know you — to name you) he exalted our own confiscated liberty and from Geneva to Algiers, from New York to Moscow, all the world's magazines reproduced these passionate stanzas. Most of the poems making up this book were reprinted in Switzerland, then again in France under the title *Dignes de Vivre.* In Geneva, in *Le Lit la Table,* he published even more eloquent poems under his own name, among them *Enterrar y Callar* inspired by Goya, and the admirable *Critique de la Poésie,* ending with this verse, blinding as a flash of fire:

Decour a été mis à mort

In February, 1944, Paul Eluard returned from the provinces where he had spent several months co-ordinating liaison between the two zones and with even more ardor again took up the struggle he had never ceased to wage. He again took up his perilous work in Paris. In June, 1944, he created the *Eternelle Revue* in which he proposed to group around himself the best of our young writers. « Once again, defiant poetry regroups, finds again an exact direction for its latent violence, cries out, accuses, and hopes. »

Today, in a free Paris, Paul Eluard, who is far from feeling himself free of all constraint and who is not ignorant of the struggles to which poets « who must fight with something other than words » are fraternally invited, does not lose hope of realizing, as in *Les Pentes Inférieures,* which he wrote at the beginning of the occupation:

> *The single dream of the innocent*
> *A single murmur a single morning*
> *And the seasons together*
> *Coloring with snow and fire*
> *A multitude at last united.*

The poet's wish is far from being fulfilled. The war goes on and we have not seen all the forms it will take. The « reign of iniquity », against which he has always stood, goes on and inspires him with more than one reaction of anger. In *Comprenne qui Voudra,* published in November, 1944, he denounces the incoherence of a justice which strikes without discernment. « I still see the lamentable idiots trembling with fear under the laughter of the mob. These girls had not sold France... In any case, they pointed a moral to no one. While the bandits with the faces of apostles have left. Though some of them, realizing their power, remain peacefully at home in the hope of starting again tomorrow. »

It is to obtain this justice, which poets rightly confuse with Poetry, that Paul Eluard is today on the side of those who wish to hasten its coming.

Again I see the poet during these past four years. I see him in the mountains of Lozère where he had fled the Gestapo. He had taken refuge in an insane asylum at Saint-Alban. These were two months of work in the course of which he wrote numerous poems inspired by the misery of the demented among whom he lived. Again I see the immense, snow-covered plateau gripped by icy whirlwinds; the high, cracked walls of the house, the haggard faces watching from the windows, the little cemetery similar to those described in our bleakest novels. Eluard left this place in the snow and cold, taking the train to the neighboring small town where he was to correct proofs. It was at Saint-Flour that he edited the *Bibliothèque Française* whose issues, undiscoverable today, may be compared to the finest realizations of the clandestine press. I see him again at Clermont-Ferrand where he stopped to seek out many friends, after meeting many more in Antibes and Villeneuve, fixing with them the main outline of a fruitful common work. Never did his certitude of a victorious outcome for the Resistance waver. On each of his trips he brought back to us new reasons for hope. And this hope which runs throughout his entire work is the same hope which inspires us today.

Louis Parrot.

XXVI

UNINTERRUPTED
POETRY

T HE *prière d'insérer* of *Poésie Ininterrompue* says
that this book contains the most « important »
of Eluard's poems; and there, surely, we have a
risky affirmation, for by what criterion could we
find, for example, a poem by Eluard *more important* than *Liberté?* But if it is a question of
understanding important in a quantitative sense,
as we might say of *consequence,* then it is true that
a poem of nearly seven hundred verses is an
unusual thing in the work of Paul Eluard; and that
Eluard, in the beginning of 1946, is risking such an
experiment in the face of modern fashion and suc-
cess, so as not to cover up the type of *importance*
of an eight-line poem such as *Couvre-Feu* in *Poésie
et Vérité* 1942 for all those who attentively follow
the progress of this free spirit (never, for his very
freedom, the fact of change or arbitrariness), it is
still in all at the bottom of a scale of importance
which is not qualified or measured.

Poetry is language, and for this reason nothing
is so necessary for a poet than first to make the
trial of language; no one was more deeply
convinced of this than Eluard in the period following the first war. In a degree, the very fact of
approaching, on the morrow of this last war, what
painters call « la grande composition » can only be
taken as a sign of resolved difficulty, as the passage

to a new stage of this poetic thought which has never yielded to facility or self-satisfaction.

It is certain that those who waited for Eluard at the turning-point following *Au Rendez-vous Allemand* secretly hoping to see the poet either beat a retreat or lose himself in the prosaic expression of reality, are doubly disconcerted and beaten. For, finally aproaching « la grande composition », Paul Eluard by his own mastered language succeeds in linking himself to the poetry of his youth, to the poetry of *Le Devoir et L'Inquiétude* and *Les Animaux et Leurs Hommes* and yet prolongs that experiment in human expression which he forged for himself in the very heart of our dangers. One may find strange the rapprochement I make between this poem and the *Geste de Peire Cardenal*. Perhaps some will understand me better if I say that I want, by relating them, to underline the permanence, through the centuries, of a certain type of poetry of which another example is the introduction to the *Chronique Rimée* of Georges Chastelain — without mentioning some poems of Pablo Neruda. A certain poetry which is like the voice of a lone man in a deserted palace adorned with high mirrors, a man whose voice is the conscience of a world of stones and echoes, a man who sees beyond the walls the hidden significance of things and who speaks, in the midst of the dumb and deaf, the very language of the future.

What does this voice say?

For the first time in a long while I am eager to make a summary of a poem as the critic does of a novel. And that is not so absurd. In another day it must have been done to *Jocelyn* or *Zim-Zimi;* why not, in our time, to *Poésie Ininterrompue?*

To whom is the first word, whose language, here feminine, perhaps distinguishes in the poet himself one of the elements of internal contradiction that he bears? Whether it is the woman or whether it is the woman in the couple...

(For in modern poetry there is this novelty, to which no one can make us return in the name of eternal Platonism; it is that man is no longer thought of without woman, nor woman without man, and that the high expression of love in these times is no longer an *idea* of love, or the unilateral expression of desire, no longer the lover but the couple; and the poetry of Eluard is fully lighted with this novelty....)

In any case, the one who speaks here *as a woman:*

Comme une femme solitaire	*Like a woman alone*
Qui dessine pour parler	*Tracing pictures in order to speak*
Dans le désert	*In the wilderness*
Et pour voir devant elle	*And to see before her*

the woman alone of all slumber yet of the man who will soon have his say; it is she who lives in the present, to whom all is present. In her mouth, the play of opposites, to which Jordi de Sant Jordi limits himself, is singularly surpassed, because the sense of this relationship is, like the couple, a recent acquisition in poetry:

Tous les mots sont d'accord	*All words are in agreement*
La boue est caressante	*The mud is caressing*
Quand la terre dégèle	*In a springtime thaw*
Le ciel est souterrain	*The sky is underground*
Quand il montre la mort	*When it shows death*
Le soir est matinal	*And evening is early*
Après un jour de peine	*After a day of sorrow*

But here is the man (*L'Homme mortel et divisé*) who « always regrets », and certainly we need

XXIX

decision and audacity to affirm that here the recitant changes, that the poet is more this man than
he was this woman, that the isolation of both
factors of the couple is not simply the liberation of
two equilibrated forces in Man (French does not
have the generic word which signifies man and
woman, as the German *mensch*). *L'homme en butte
au passé* then, for whom the problem is:

Savoir vieillir savoir passer le temps	To know how to grow old to know how to pass the time

In his speech the very tenses of the verbs vary,
with this strangeness sometimes reached by Apol-
linaire in *Le Larron* or *L'Emigrant du Landor
Road. Le chapeau à la main il entra du pied
droit...* Syntax serves Eluard, by returning from
the present indicative to the definite past, for com-
municating to us the bitterness of growing old.

L'on m'aimera car j'aime par-dessus tout ordre	I shall be loved for I love above all order
Et je suis prêt à tout pour l'avenir de tous	I am ready for all for the future of all
Et je ne connais rien de rien à l'avenir	I know nothing of anything in the future
Mais j'aime pour aimer et je mourrai d'amour	But I love for the sake of loving and I shall die of love
Il se mit à genoux pour un premier baiser	He fell on his knees for one first kiss
La nuit était pareille à la nuit d'autrefois	Night like the night of another time
Et ce fut le départ et la fin du passé	This was the parting the finish of the past

But I have scarcely started on this interpretation
when a chance quotation reveals to me, in the
envisaged couple, the perspective of entire humanity. It is the love-language of man and woman,

XXX

with its oppositions, its contradictory play, but the profound will of the poem breaks out almost immediately. Which is the resolution of these contradictions in the love of all men, of the man:

Et je suis prêt à tout pour l'avenir de tous	*I am ready for all for the future of all*

Here too is one of the universal characteristics of modern love, which is the object of the new poetry and by this is opposed to the conception of the *amour provençal* of Nelli: that the love of man and woman in the couple finds its harmony precisely when the man and woman rise simultaneously to the same conception of the world, where their adventure widens and the love of human becoming identifies itself.

And if, a little while back, you were able to doubt the meaning of the feminine language, if you were able to hesitate as if before a rhetorical device, before the feminine given to adjectives accompanying him or her who spoke in the first person, and you were still able to wonder whether you had dealings with an image or a woman, now in the man's speech, when it is to whom the recitant addresses himself that the grammatical attributes of femininity are devolved, you know with a sure knowledge that is the woman to whom the man is speaking that it is his wife to whom the poet speaks, to his wife, the be-all and end-all of his life and his reason for being*.

Que ma parole pèse sur la nuit qui passe	*May my word weigh on the passing night*
Et que s'ouvre toujours la porte par laquelle	*And may the door be ever open*

---

* And not to the idea of woman, minuscule, never seen, invented, forgotten...

XXXI

Tu es entré dans ce poème	*By which you entered in this poem*
Porte de ton sourire et porte de ton corps	*Door of your smile your body's door*

And it is from this newly found certitude that we mark the starting point of what is at once resolution and crowning point of the poem whose design is here confessed:

Mais il nous faut encore un peu	*But we need a little more*
Accorder nos yeux clairs à ces nuits inhumaines	*To reconcile our clear eyes to these inhuman nights*
Des hommes qui n'ont pas trouvé la vie sur terre	*Of men who have not found a life on earth*
Il nous faut qualifier leur sort pour les sauver	*We must qualify their fate to save them*

Here something begins which cannot be summarized. From the depths of night... yet I was going to attempt a resumé of it, and in the very words of a *De Profundis* which believes in man and not in God. It is a poem in distiches, at first heptasyllabic, which rises from the depths of all sorts of nights, from the depths of misery, massacres, shabbiness, insignificance, luxury, pessimism... interrupting itself like a spoken phrase

Si nous montions d'un degré	*If we go up one degree*

which repeats itself in vain, which is not a refrain but a march, and the double beating of the couplets draws us through this lightless world:

Vers la plainte d'un berger	*To the complaint of a shepherd*
Qui est seul et qui a froid	*Cold and alone*

XXXII

Vers une main généreuse	*To a generous hand*
Qui se tend et que l'on souille	*Extended and spat upon*
Vers un aveugle humilié	*To a blindman humiliated*
De se cogner aux fenêtres	*By stumbling against windows*

And we go up one degree, believe me, just when the poem to this terrible world *sticks* and here, to this terrible world is the terrible scanned song:

Les guerres s'immobilisent	*Wars immobilise themselves*
Sur les glaciers opulents	*On opulent glaciers*
Entre les armes en brouis-sailles	*Meat and blood parch*
Sèchent la viande et le sang	*Between brushwood weapons*
De quoi calmer les âmes amoureuses	*The wherewithal to calm the amorous souls*
De quoi varier le cours des rêveries	*The wherewithal to change the course of reveries*
De quoi provoquer l'oubli	*The wherewithal to breed oblivion*
Aussi de quoi changer la loi	*Also the wherewithal to change the law*
La loi la raison pratique	*The law the practical reason*
Et que comprendre juge	*Let understanding judge*
L'erreur selon l'ereur	*Error according to error*
Si voir était la foudre	*If seeing were the lightning*
Au pays de charogne	*In the land of carrion*
Le juge serait dieu	*The judge would be god*
Il n'y a pas de dieu	*There is no god*

I beg you, understand all this as if it were written in a newspaper. They say the war is over, but the bloody victims still stink in the universe, less

XXXIII

than the criminals already forgotten. Read this in the great hours of Nuremberg when the gentlemen of the *Figaro* are already tired of our continuing to remember French crime... Eluard is not speaking in the moon, all this is really the earth on which we want that « understanding judge error according to error », Pétain according to the law of Pétain, Brasillach and Goering according to Brasillach and Goering, but: *if we go up one degree?*

Et nous montons	*And we go higher*

Yes, throughout this poem we go up by degrees which I shall not make you follow toward this moral of Eluard's poetry (« I was born to know you — To name you — Liberty ») which of course can appear only with the characteristics of another year when we truly believed the moral born from earth.

Et c'est très vite	*And it's very quick*
La liberté conquise	*Liberty conquered*
. . . .	. . . .
Et les hommes dehors	*And the men outside*
Et les hommes partout	*And the men everywhere*
Tenant toute la place	*Holding all places*
Abattant les murailles	*Breaking down the walls*
Se partageant le pain	*Sharing the bread*
Dévêtant le soleil	*Unveiling the sun*

Here the poem becomes a canticle and ends in the fulfillment of the couple in which it takes its origin and sap:

Nous deux nous ne vivons	*And we two we live only*
que pour être fidèles	*to be faithful*
A la vie	*To life*

Poésie Ininterrompue is not only this poem, it is a book — and not a chance composition, an anthology. The five other poems* which complete this great initial work may be separated by their subject matter, but they are animated by the same spirit, they are moments of the same quest, in which denunciation of the world as it is, of the black world, is reached by a call from a different world, by negation of the original pessimism:

Je sais parce que je le dis	I know because I say it
Que ma colère a raison	That my rage is right
Le ciel a été foulé la chair	The sky has been down-
de l'homme	trodden the flesh of man
A été mise en pièces	Cut into tiny pieces
Glacée soumise dispersée	Frozen submissive and dis-
	persed

Je veux qu'on lui rende jus-	I want him to be given
tice	justice
Une justice sans pitié	A justice without pity
Et que l'on frappe en plein	I want the butchers struck
visage des bourreaux	full in the face
Les maîtres sans racines	The rootless masters among
parmi nous **	us

Read that like a newspaper, I beg you, in the great hours of Nuremberg. Poetry reads like a newspaper, not only in the hours of Nuremberg but in the great hours of an entire world...

Je sais parce que je le dis	I know because I say it
Que mon désespoir a tort	That my despair is wrong
Il y a partout des ventres	Everywhere there are ten-
tendres	der wombs
Pour inventer des hommes	To invent men
Pareils à moi	Like unto me
Mon orgeuil n'a pas tort	My pride is not wrong

---

* *Moralité du Sommeil, Le Travail du Poète, Le Travail du Peintre, A l'Echelle Animale, L'Age de la Vie.* — Tr.

** The concluding stanzas of *Le Travail du Poète.* — Tr.

Le monde ancien ne peut
me toucher je suis libre
Je ne suis pas un fils de
roi je suis un homme
Debout qu'on a voulu abat-
tre

The old world cannot
touch me I am free
I am no king's son I am
a man
Still standing where they
would have struck me
down

Read that like a newspaper. Poetry, our poetry, reads like a newspaper. The news of a world to come.

ARAGON.

XXXVI

TRANSLATOR'S NOTE

Translating poetry is as risky as playing music. Like the performer, the translator may gain his own special sense of inner voices and structures; but the rewards of insight are no protection against the hazards of execution. Working closely with the poetry of Paul Eluard has allowed me to marvel at it all the more, and also has made me all the more aware of its difficulties for the translator. Essence, poetic or musical, can be often elusive. As with all true poets, Eluard's passion, compassion, and vision are inseparable from the unique qualities of his diction. In another language, these qualities may at best be suggested, seldom perfectly duplicated. I hope these English versions will be satisfying in themselves; but, more important, I hope they will guide the reader to the richness of the originals.

From our first meeting in Paris in 1946 until his death in 1952, Paul Eluard gave me welcome guidance, encouragement, and friendship. To this note, I add my continuing gratitude and appreciation.

L. A.

POEMES

Le cœur sur l'arbre vous n'aviez qu'à le cueillir,
Sourire et rire, rire et douceur d'outre-sens.
Vaincu, vainqueur et lumineux, pur comme un
    ange,
Haut vers le ciel, avec les arbres.

Au loin, geint une belle qui voudrait lutter
Et qui ne peut, couchée au pied de la colline.
Et que le ciel soit misérable ou transparent
On ne peut la voir sans l'aimer.

Les jours comme des doigts repliant leurs pha-
    langes.
Les fleurs sont desséchées, les graines sont perdues,
La canicule attend les grandes gelées blanches.

A l'œil du pauvre mort. Peindre des porcelaines.
Une musique, bras blancs tout nus.
Les vents et les oiseaux s'unissent — le ciel change.

⊙

POEMES POUR LA PAIX

Toutes les femmes heureuses ont
Retrouvé leur mari — il revient du soleil
Tant il apporte de chaleur.
Il rit et dit bonjour tout doucement
Avant d'embrasser sa merveille.

2

POEMS

The heart on the tree you had only to pluck it,
Smile and laughter, laughter and sweetness of the
　　furthest senses.
Conquered, conquering and luminous, pure as an
　　angel,
High toward heaven, with the trees.

From afar, moans a lovely woman who would like
　　to struggle
And who cannot, lying at the foot of the hill.
And whether the sky be wretched or transparent
You cannot see her without loving her.

The days like fingers coiling their knuckles.
The flowers have dried out, the seeds are lost,
The dog days await the great white frosts.

In the eye of a poor corpse. To paint porcelains.
An air of music, white arms all naked.
The winds and birds unite — the sky changes.

⊙

POEMS FOR PEACE

All the happy women have
Found their husbands again — he might be return-
　　ing from the sun
So much warmth he brings.
He laughs and says good morning softly
Before kissing his marvel.

Splendide, la poitrine cambrée légèrement
Sainte ma femme, tu es à moi bien mieux qu'au
    temps
Où avec lui, et lui, et lui, et lui, et lui,
Je tenais un fusil, un bidon — notre vie!

J'ai eu longtemps un visage inutile,
Mais maintenant
J'ai un visage pour être aimé
J'ai un visage pour être heureux.

Je rêve de toutes les belles
Qui se promènent dans la nuit,
Très calmes,
Avec la lune qui voyage.

Toute la fleur des fruits éclaire mon jardin,
Les arbres de beauté et les arbres fruitiers
Et je travaille et je suis seul en mon jardin,
Et le Soleil brûle en feu sombre sur mes mains.

⊙

L'AMOUREUSE

Elle est debout sur mes paupières
Et ses cheveux sont dans les miens,
Elle a la forme de mes mains,
Elle a la couleur de mes yeux,
Elle s'engloutit dans mon ombre
Comme une pierre sur le ciel.

Splendid, the breast lightly arched
Saint of a wife, you are mine much better than
     when
With him, and him, and him, and him, and him,
I held a rifle, a canteen — our life!

For a long while I had a useless face,
But now
I have a face for being loved
I have a face for being happy.

I dream of all the lovely women
Who walk in the night
Very calm,
With the voyaging moon.

All the fruit blossoms brighten my garden,
Trees of beauty and trees of fruit
And I work and I am alone in my garden,
And the Sun burns in somber fire on my hands.

⊙

WOMAN IN LOVE

She is standing on my eyelids
And her hair is in mine,
She has the shape of my hands,
She has the color of my eyes,
She is engulfed in my shadow
Like a stone against the sky.

Elle a toujours les yeux ouverts
Et ne me laisse pas dormir.
Ses rêves en pleine lumière
Font s'évaporer les soleils,
Me font rire, pleurer et rire,
Parler sans avoir rien à dire.

⊙

PREMIERE DU MONDE

à Pablo Picasso

Captive de la plaine, agonisante folle,
La lumière sur toi se cache, vois le ciel :
Il a fermé les yeux pour s'en prendre à ton rêve,
Il a fermé ta robe pour briser tes chaînes.

Devant les roues toutes nouées
Un éventail rit aux éclats.
Dans les traîtres filets de l'herbe
Les routes perdent leur reflet.

Ne peux-tu donc prendre les vagues
Dont les barques sont les amandes
Dans ta paume chaude et câline
Ou dans les boucles de ta tête ?

Ne peux-tu prendre les étoiles ?
Ecartelée tu leur ressembles,
Dans leur nid de feu tu demeures
Et ton éclat s'en multiplie.

6

[1924-1926]

Her eyes are always open
She does not let me sleep.
Her dreams in broad daylight
Make suns evaporate,
Make me laugh, weep and laugh,
And speak without anything to say.

⊙

FIRST IN THE WORLD

To Pablo Picasso

Captive of the plain, madwoman in agony,
Light hides on you, behold the sky:
It has closed its eyes to enter your dream,
It has fastened your dress to break your chains.

Before the knotted wheels
A fan bursts into laughter.
In the traitor nets of grass
The roads lose their reflection.

Can you not take the waves
Where ships are almonds
In your hot coaxing palm
Or in the curls of your head?

Can you not take the stars?
Spread out you resemble them,
You dwell in their nest of fire
And your brilliance is multiplied by it.

7

De l'aube bâillonnée un seul cri veut jaillir,
Un soleil tournoyant ruisselle sous l'écorce,
Il ira se fixer sur tes paupières closes.
O douce, quand tu dors, la nuit se mêle au jour.

⊙

LA DAME DE CARREAU

Tout jeune, j'ai ouvert mes bras à la pureté. Ce ne fut qu'un battement d'ailes au ciel de mon éternité, qu'un battement de cœur amoureux qui bat dans les poitrines conquises. Je ne pouvais plus tomber.

Aimant l'amour. En vérité, la lumière m'éblouit. J'en garde assez en moi pour regarder la nuit, toute la nuit, toutes les nuits.

Toutes les vierges sont différentes. Je rêve toujours d'une vierge.

A l'école, elle est au banc devant moi, en tablier noir. Quand elle se retourne pour me demander la solution d'un problème, l'innocence de ses yeux me confond à un tel point que, prenant mon trouble en pitié, elle passe ses bras autour de mon cou.

Ailleurs, elle me quitte. Elle monte sur un bateau. Nous sommes presque étrangers l'un à l'autre, mais sa jeunesse est si grande que son baiser ne me surprend point.

Ou bien, quand elle est malade, c'est sa main que je garde dans les miennes, jusqu'à en mourir, jusqu'à m'éveiller.

Je cours d'autant plus vite à ses rendez-vous que j'ai peur de n'avoir pas le temps d'arriver avant que d'autres pensées me dérobent à moi-même.

Une fois, le monde allait finir et nous ignorions

8

[1926]

From stifled dawn one cry alone will burst,
And spinning sunlight streams beneath the bark,
And it will come to rest upon your closed eyelids.
O sweet one, when you sleep, the night is mixed
    with day.

☉

THE QUEEN OF DIAMONDS

When I was young, I opened my arms to purity.
This was only a beating of wings in the sky of my
eternity, only a beating of the loving heart which
beats in conquered breasts. I could fall no more.

Loving love. Actually, light dazzles me. I keep
only enough of it in me to look at night, the whole
night, all nights.

All virgins are different. I always dream of a
virgin.

At school, she is on the bench in front of me,
wearing a black apron. When she turns to ask me
the solution of a problem, the innocence of her eyes
confuses me to such a point that, taking pity on my
discomfort, she puts her arms around my neck.

Elsewhere, she leaves me. She gets on a ship. We
are almost strangers one to the other, but her
youth is so great that her kiss does not surprise me
at all.

Or, when she is sick, I hold her hand in mine,
until death, until awakening.

I run all the more quickly to meet her since I
am afraid of not having time to get there before
other thoughts steal me from myself.

Once, the world was going to end and we knew

tout de notre amour. Elle a cherché mes lèvres avec des mouvements de tête lents et caressants. J'ai bien cru, cette nuit-là, que je la ramènerais au jour.

Et c'est toujours le même aveu, la même jeunesse, les mêmes yeux purs, le même geste ingénu de ses bras autour de mon cou, la même caresse, la même révélation.

Mais ce n'est jamais la même femme.

Les cartes ont dit que je la rencontrerai dans la vie, *mais sans la reconnaître.*

Aimant l'amour.

⊙

A LA FENETRE

Je n'ai pas toujours eu cette sûreté, ce pessimisme qui rassure les meilleurs d'entre nous. Il fut un temps où mes amis riaient de moi. Je n'étais pas le maître de mes paroles. Une certaine indifférence. Je n'ai pas toujours bien su ce que je voulais dire, mais, le plus souvent, c'est que je n'avais rien à dire. La nécessité de parler et le désir de n'être pas entendu. Ma vie ne tenant qu'à un fil.

Il fut un temps où je ne semblais rien comprendre. Mes chaînes flottaient sur l'eau.

Tous mes désirs sont nés de mes rêves. Et j'ai prouvé mon amour avec des mots. A quelle créature fantastique me suis-je donc confié, dans quel monde douloureux et ravissant mon imagination m'a-t-elle enfermé ? Je suis sûr d'avoir été aimé dans le plus mystérieux des domaines, le mien. Le langage de mon amour n'appartient pas au langage

10

nothing at all of our love. She sought my lips with
slow and caressing movements of her head. That
night I really thought I would bring her back to
daylight.

And it is always the same confession, the same
youth, the same pure eyes, the same ingenuous
gesture of her arms about my neck, the same
caress, the same revelation.

But it is never the same woman.

The cards have said that I would meet her in
life, *but without recognising her.*

Loving love.

⊙

AT THE WINDOW

I have not always had this certainty, this
pessimism which reassures the best among us.
There was a time when my friends laughed at me.
I was not the master of my words. A certain indif-
ference. I have not always known well what I
wanted to say, but most often it was because I had
nothing to say. The necessity of speaking and the
desire not to be heard. My life hanging only by a
thread.

There was a time when I seemed to understand
nothing. My chains floated on the water.

All my desires are born of my dreams. And I
have proven my love with words. To what fantastic
creatures have I entrusted myself, in what dolorous
and ravishing world has my imagination enclosed
me ? I am sure of having been loved in the most
mysterious of domains, my own. The language of
my love does not belong to human language, my

humain, mon corps humain ne touche pas à la chair de mon amour. Mon imagination amoureuse a toujours été assez constante et assez haute pour que nul ne puisse tenter de me convaincre d'erreur.

⊙

PREMIEREMENT

Je te l'ai dit pour les nuages
Je te l'ai dit pour l'arbre de la mer
Pour chaque vague pour les oiseaux dans les
    feuilles
Pour les cailloux du bruit
Pour les mains familières
Pour l'œil qui devient visage ou paysage
Et le sommeil lui rend le ciel de sa couleur
Pour toute la nuit bue
Pour la grille des routes
Pour la fenêtre ouverte pour un front découvert
Je te l'ai dit pour tes pensées pour tes paroles
Toute caresse toute confiance se survivent.

Toi la seule et j'entends les herbes de ton rire
Toi c'est ta tête qui t'enlève
Et du haut des dangers de mort

Sous les globes brouillés de la pluie des vallées
Sous la lumière lourde sous le ciel de terre
Tu enfantes la chute.

Les oiseaux ne sont plus un abri suffisant
Ni la paresse ni la fatigue
Le souvenir des bois et des ruisseaux fragiles
Au matin des caprices

12

human body does not touch the flesh of my love.
My amorous imagination has always been constant
and high enough so that nothing could attempt to
convince me of error.

⊙

FIRSTLY

I told it to you for the clouds
I told it to you for the tree of the sea
For every wave for birds in the leaves
For pebbles of sound
For familiar hands
For the eye which becomes face or landscape
And sleep gives back to it the sky of its color
For all the night drunk
For the network of roads
For the open window for a discovered brow
I told it to you for your thoughts your words
And each caress each confidence survives.

You alone and I hear the grass of your laughter
You it is your head which carries you away
And above the dangers of death

Under the confused globes of the valleys' rain
Under the heavy light under the sky of earth
You give birth to the fall.

The birds no longer are sufficient shelter
Nor idleness nor fatigue
The memory of woods and fragile rivulets
In the morning of caprice

13

Au matin des caresses visibles
Au grand matin de l'absence la chute.

Les barques de tes yeux s'égarent
Dans la dentelle des disparitions
Le gouffre est dévoilé aux autres de l'éteindre
Les ombres que tu crées n'ont pas droit à la nuit.

Mon amour pour avoir figuré mes désirs
Mis tes lèvres au ciel de tes mots comme un astre
Tes baisers dans la nuit vivante
Et le sillage de tes bras autour de moi
Comme une flamme en signe de conquête
Mes rêves sont au monde
Clairs et perpétuels.

Et quand tu n'es pas là
Je rêve que je dors je rêve que je rêve.

D'une seule caresse
Je te fais briller de tout ton éclat.

⊙

NUITS PARTAGEES

Au terme d'un long voyage, je revois toujours ce corridor, cette taupe, cette ombre chaude à qui l'écume de mer prescrit des courants d'air purs comme de tout petits enfants, je revois toujours la chambre où je venais rompre avec toi le pain de nos désirs, je revois toujours ta pâleur dévêtue qui, le matin, fait corps avec les étoiles qui disparaissent. Je sais que je vais encore fermer les yeux pour retrouver les couleurs et les formes conven-

[1929-1932]

In the morning of visible caresses
In the full morning of absence the fall.

The ships of your eyes are lost
In the lace of disappearances
The chasm is revealed for others to extinguish
The shadows you create have no right to the night.

My love for having figured my desires
Placed your lips in the sky of your words as a star
Your kisses in the living night
And the wake of your arms about me
Like a flame in sign of conquest
My dreams are in the world
Clear and perpetual.

And when you are not there
I dream that I sleep I dream that I dream.

With a single caress
I make you burn in all your brilliance.

⊙

SHARED NIGHTS

At the end of a long voyage, I see again this
corridor, this mole, this hot shadow for which sea
foam prescribes currents of air pure as tiny children,
I see again the room where I came to break
with you the bread of our desires, I see again
your undressed pallor which, in the morning,
makes body with the disappearing stars. I know
that I am again going to close my eyes in order to
find the conventional colors and forms which allow

tionnelles qui me permettent de t'aborder. Quand je les rouvrirai, ce sera pour chercher dans un coin l'ombrelle corruptible à manche de pioche qui me fait redouter le beau temps, le soleil, la vie, car je ne t'aime plus au grand jour, car je regrette le temps où j'étais parti à ta découverte et le temps aussi où j'étais aveugle et muet devant l'univers incompréhensible et le système d'entente incohérent que tu me proposais.

N'as-tu pas suffisamment porté la responsabilité de cette candeur qui m'obligeait à toujours retourner tes volontés contre toi ?

Que ne m'as-tu donné à penser ! Maintenant, je ne viens plus te voir que pour être plus sûr du grand mystère qui constitue encore l'absurde durée de ma vie, l'absurde durée d'une nuit.

Quand j'arrive, toutes les barques s'en vont, l'orage recule devant elles. Une ondée délivre les fleurs obscures, leur éclat recommence et frappe de nouveau les murs de laine. Je sais, tu n'es jamais sûre de rien, mais l'idée du mensonge, mais l'idée d'une erreur sont tellement au-dessus de nos forces. Il y a si longtemps que la porte têtue n'avait pas cédé, si longtemps que la monotonie de l'espoir nourrissait l'ennui, si longtemps que tes sourires étaient des larmes.

Nous avons refusé de laisser entrer les spectateurs, car il n'y a pas de spectacle. Souviens-toi, pour la solitude, la scène vide, sans décors, sans acteurs, sans musiciens. L'on dit : le théâtre du monde, la scène mondiale et, nous deux, nous ne savons plus ce que c'est. Nous deux, j'insiste sur ces mots, car aux étapes de ces longs voyages que nous faisions séparément, je le sais maintenant, nous étions vraiment ensemble, nous étions vraiment, nous étions, nous. Ni toi, ni moi ne savions ajouter

me to approach you. When I open them again, it
will be to seek in a corner the corruptible parasol
with a pick handle that makes me dread fair
weather, sunshine, life, for no longer do I love you
in broad daylight, because I regret the time when
I left for your discovery and as well the time when
I was blind and dumb before the incomprehensible
universe and the system of incoherent understanding you proposed to me.

Have you not sufficiently borne the responsibility of this candor which obliged me always to turn
your wishes against you?

What have you not given me to think about! Now,
no longer do I come to see you but to be more sure
of the great mystery that still constitutes the absurd
duration of my life, the absurd duration of a night.

When I arrive, all the ships sail away, the storm
falls back before them. A shower delivers the
obscure flowers, their brilliance revives and strikes
again the woolen walls. I know, you are never
sure of anything, but the idea of a lie, the idea
of an error are so far beyond our strength. It was
such a long time ago that the stubborn door had
not yielded, such a long time ago that the mono-
tony of hope nourished boredom, such a long time
ago that your smiles were tears.

We have refused to let spectators enter, for there
is no show. Remember, for solitude, the empty
stage, without scenery, without actors, without
musicians. They say : the theatre of the world,
the world stage, and we two, we no longer know
what it is. We two, I insist on these words, for in
the stages of those long voyages we made sepa-
rately, I know now, we were really together, we were
truly, we were, we. Neither you nor I knew how to
add the time which had separated us to this time

17

le temps qui nous avait séparés à ce temps pendant lequel nous étions réunis, ni toi, ni moi ne savions l'en soustraire.

Une ombre chacun, mais dans l'ombre nous l'oublions.

La lumière m'a pourtant donné de belles images des négatifs de nos rencontres. Je t'ai identifiée à des êtres dont seule la variété justifiait le nom, toujours le même, le tien, dont je voulais les nommer, des êtres que je transformais comme je te transformais, en pleine lumière, comme on transforme l'eau d'une source en la prenant dans un verre, comme on transforme sa main en la mettant dans une autre. La neige même, qui fut derrière nous l'écran douloureux sur lequel les cristaux des serments fondaient, la neige même était masquée. Dans les cavernes terrestres, des plantes cristallisées cherchaient les décolletés de la sortie.

Ténèbres abyssales toutes tendues vers une confusion éblouissante, je ne m'apercevais pas que ton nom devenait illusoire, qu'il n'était plus que sur ma bouche et que, peu à peu, le visage des tentations apparaissait réel, entier, seul. C'est alors que je me retournais vers toi.

Réunis, chaque fois à jamais réunis, ta voix comble tes yeux comme l'écho comble le ciel du soir. Je descends vers les rivages de ton apparence. Que dis-tu ? Que tu n'a jamais cru être seule, que tu n'as pas rêvé depuis que je t'ai vue, que tu es comme une pierre que l'on casse pour avoir deux pierres plus belles que leur mère morte, que tu étais la femme d'hier et que tu es la femme d'aujourd'hui, qu'il n'y a pas à te consoler puisque tu t'es divisée pour être intacte à l'heure qu'il est.

Toute nue, toute nue, tes seins sont plus fragiles

18

during which we were reunited, neither you nor I knew how to subtract from it.

Each one a shadow, but in the shadow we forget it.

Yet the light has given me beautiful pictures from the negatives of our meetings. I have identified you with beings whose variety alone justified their name, always the same, your own, with which I wanted to name them, beings I transformed as I transformed you, in full light, as one transforms the water of a spring by taking it in a glass, as one transforms his hand by putting it in another. Even the snow, which behind us was the dolorous screen on which the crystal of pledges melted, even the snow was masked. In earthly caverns, crystallized plants sought the neckline of the way out.

Abysmal shadows all stretched toward a dazzling confusion, I did not perceive that your name was becoming illusory, that it was only on my lips and that, little by little, the visage of temptations appeared real, entire, alone. It was then that I turned back toward you.

Reunited, each time forever reunited, your voice fills your eyes as the echo fills the evening sky. I descend toward the riverbanks of your appearance. What are you saying? That you have never thought to be alone, that you have never dreamed since I saw you, that you are like a stone broken to make two stones more lovely than their dead mother, that you were the woman of yesterday and that you are the woman of today, that there is no need to console you since you divided yourself in order to be intact at this time.

All naked, all naked, your breasts are more

que le parfum de l'herbe gelée et ils supportent tes épaules. Toute nue. Tu enlèves ta robe avec la plus grande simplicité. Et tu fermes les yeux et c'est la chute d'une ombre sur un corps, la chute de l'ombre tout entière sur les dernières flammes.

Les gerbes des saisons s'écroulent, tu me montres le fond de ton cœur. C'est la lumière de la vie qui profite des flammes qui s'abaissent, c'est une oasis qui profite du désert que le désert féconde, que la désolation nourrit. La fraîcheur délicate et creuse se substitue aux foyers tournoyants qui te mettaient en tête de me désirer. Au-dessus de toi, ta chevelure glisse dans l'abîme qui justifie notre éloignement.

Que ne puis-je encore, comme au temps de ma jeunesse, me déclarer ton disciple, que ne puis-je encore convenir avec toi que le couteau et ce qu'il coupe sont bien accordés. Le piano et le silence, l'horizon et l'étendue.

Par ta force et par ta faiblesse, tu croyais pouvoir concilier les désaccords de la présence et les harmonies de l'absence, une union maladroite, naïve, et la science des privations. Mais, plus bas que tout, il y avait l'ennui. Que veux-tu que cet aigle aux yeux crevés retienne de nos nostalgies ?

Dans les rues, dans les campagnes, cent femmes sont dispersées par toi, tu déchires la ressemblance qui les lie, cent femmes sont réunies par toi et tu ne peux leur donner de nouveaux traits communs et elles ont cent visages, cent visages qui tiennent ta beauté en échec.

Et dans l'unité d'un temp partagé, il y eut soudain tel jour de telle année que je ne pus accepter.

fragile than the perfume of frozen grass and they support your shoulders. All naked. You remove your dress with the greatest simplicity. And you close your eyes and it is the fall of a shadow on a body, the fall of the entire shadow on the last flames.

The sheaves of the seasons crumble, you show me the bottom of your heart. It is the light of life which profits of the dying flames, it is an oasis which profits of the desert, that the desert fertilizes, that desolation nourishes. Delicate and hollow freshness is substituted for the swirling hearths which gave you the idea of desiring me. Above you, your hair slips into the abyss which justifies our remoteness.

Why can I not again, as in the time of. my youth, declare myself your disciple, why can I not again acknowledge with you that the knife and what it cuts are quite in accordance. The piano and the silence, the horizon and the extent.

By your strength and by your weakness you thought you could reconcile the discords of presence and the harmonies of absence, a clumsy, naive union, and the science of privations. But, lower than all, was weariness. How do you expect this eagle with its eyes torn out to retain our nostalgias ?

In the streets, in the country, a hundred women are dispersed by you, you rend the resemblance that binds them, a hundred women are reunited by you and you can not give them new common features and they have a hundred faces, a hundred faces which hold your beauty in check.

And in the unity of a shared time, suddenly there was a certain day of a certain year that I

Tous les autres jours, toutes les autres nuits, mais ce jour-là j'ai trop souffert. La vie, l'amour avaient perdu leur point de fixation. Rassure-toi, ce n'est pas au profit de quoi que ce soit de durable que j'ai désespéré de notre entente. Je n'ai pas imaginé une autre vie devant d'autres bras, dans d'autres bras. Je n'ai pas pensé que je cesserais un jour de t'être fidèle, puisqu'à tout jamais j'avais compris ta pensée et la pensée que tu existes, que tu ne cesses d'exister qu'avec moi.

J'ai dit à des femmes que je n'aimais pas que leur existence dépendait de la tienne.

Et la vie, pourtant, s'en prenait à notre amour. La vie sans cesse à la recherche d'un nouvel amour, pour effacer l'amour ancien, l'amour dangereux, la vie voulait changer d'amour.

Principes de la fidélité... Car les principes ne dépendent pas toujours de règles sèchement inscrites sur le bois blanc des ancêtres, mais de charmes bien vivants, de regards, d'attitudes, de paroles et des signes de la jeunesse, de la pureté, de la passion. Rien de tout cela ne s'efface.

Je m'obstine à mêler des fictions aux redoutables réalités. Maisons inhabitées, je vous ai peuplées de femmes exceptionnelles, ni grasses, ni maigres, ni blondes, ni brunes, ni folles, ni sages, peu importe, de femmes plus séduisantes que possibles, par un détail. Objets inutiles, même la sottise qui procéda à votre fabrication me fut une source d'enchantements. Etres indifférents, je vous ai souvent écoutés, comme on écoute le bruit des vagues et le bruit des machines d'un bateau, en attendant délicieusement le mal de mer. J'ai pris l'habitude des images les plus inhabituelles. Je les ai vues où elles n'étaient pas. Je les ai mécanisées comme mes levers et mes couchers. Les places, comme des

could not accept. All the other days, all the other nights, but that day I suffered too much. Life, love had lost their point of fixation. Be assured, it is not for the profit of anything durable that I despaired of our understanding. I have not imagined another life before other arms, in other arms. I did not think that one day I would cease being faithful to you, since I had always understood your thoughts and the thought that you exist, that you cease to exist only with me.

I have told women that I did not like their existence depending on your own.

Still, life blamed our love. Life unceasingly searching for a new love, to obliterate the old love, the dangerous love, life wanted to change love.

Principles of fidelity... For the principles do not always depend on rules dryly inscribed on the white wood of ancestors, but on living charms, looks, attitudes, words and signs of youth, of purity, of passion. Nothing of all that is effaced.

I persist in mixing fictions with dreadful realities. Uninhabited houses, I have peopled you with exceptional women, neither fat nor thin, neither blonde nor brunette, neither mad nor wise, what matter, the most seductive women possible, by a detail. Useless objects, even the stupidity which led to your fabrication was a source of enchantment to me. Indifferent beings, I have often listened to you as one listens to the noise of waves and the noise of the engines of a ship, deliciously awaiting seasickness. I have taken the habit of the most unaccustomed images. I have seen them where they were not. I have mechanized them as my awakenings and slumberings. The squares, like

bulles de savon, ont été soumises au gonflement de mes joues, les rues à mes pieds l'un devant l'autre et l'autre passe devant l'un, devant deux et fait le total, les femmes ne se déplaçaient plus que couchées, leur corsage ouvert représentant le soleil. La raison, la tête haute, son carcan d'indifférence, lanterne à tête de fourmi, la raison, pauvre mât de fortune pour un homme affolé, le mât de fortune du bateau... voir plus haut.

Pour me trouver des raisons de vivre, j'ai tenté de détruire mes raisons de t'aimer. Pour me trouver des raisons de t'aimer, j'ai mal vécu.

Au terme d'un long voyage, peut-être n'irai-je plus vers cette porte que nous connaissons tous deux si bien, je n'entrerai peut-être plus dans cette chambre où le désespoir et le désir d'en finir avec le désespoir m'ont tant de fois attiré. A force d'être un homme incapable de surmonter son ignorance de lui-même et du destin, je prendrai peut-être parti des êtres différents de celui que j'avais inventé.

A quoi leur servirai-je ?

⊙

TU ES PARTOUT

Tu te lèves l'eau se déplie
Tu te couches l'eau s'épanouit

Tu es l'eau détournée de ses abîmes
Tu es la terre qui prend racine
Et sur laquelle tout s'établit

24

soap bubbles, have been submitted to the swelling
of my cheeks, the streets to my feet one before the
other and the other passes before the one, before
two and makes the total, women displaced themselves only in bed, their open corsage representing
the sun. Reason, the head high, its pillory of in-
difference, lantern with an ant's head, reason, poor
makeshift mast for a maddened man, the makeshift
mast of a ship... see above.

In order to find for myself reasons for living, I
attempted to destroy my reasons for loving you.
In order to find for myself reasons for loving you,
I have lived badly.

At the end of a long voyage, perhaps I shall no
longer go towards this door which we both know
so well, perhaps I shall no longer enter this room
where despair and the desire to put an end to
despair have drawn me so many times. By being
a man incapable of surmounting his ignorance of
himself and of destiny, perhaps I shall take sides
for the beings different from the one I had invented.

What good will I be to them ?

⊙

YOU ARE EVERYWHERE

You get up the water unfolds
You lie down the water expands

You are water diverted from its abysses
You are the earth which takes root
And upon which everything is built

25

Tu fais des bulles de silence dans le désert des
    bruits
Tu chantes des hymnes nocturnes sur les cordes de
    l'arc-en-ciel
Tu es partout tu abolis toutes les routes

Tu sacrifies le temps
A l'éternelle jeunesse de la flamme exacte
Qui voile la nature en la reproduisant

Femme tu mets au monde un corps toujours pareil
Le tien

Tu es la ressemblance.

⊙

POEME

On ne peut me connaître
Mieux que tu me connais

Tes yeux dans lesquels nous dormons
Tous les deux
Ont fait à mes lumières d'homme
Un sort meilleur qu'aux nuits du monde

Tes yeux dans lesquels je voyage
Ont donné aux gestes des routes
Un sens détaché de la terre

Dans tes yeux ceux qui nous révèlent
Notre solitude infinie
Ne sont plus ce qu'ils croyaient être

[1935-1936]

You blow bubbles of silence in the wilderness of
    noise
You sing nocturnal hymns on the rainbow's strings
You are everywhere you abolish all roads

You sacrifice time
To the eternal youth of the rigorous flame
Which veils nature in reproducing it

Woman you bring into the world a body always the
    same
Your own

You are its resemblance.

      ⊙

POEM

No one can know me
Better than you know me

Your eyes in which we sleep
We two
Have made for my man's lights
A destiny better than the nights of the world

Your eyes in which I voyage
Have given the movements of the roads
A direction detached from the earth

In your eyes those who reveal to us
Our infinite solitude
Are no longer what they thought themselves to be

27

On ne peut te connaître
Mieux que je te connais.

⊙

A PABLO PICASSO

I

Bonne journée j'ai revu qui je n'oublie pas
Qui je n'oublierai jamais
Et des femmes fugaces dont les yeux
Me faisaient une haie d'honneur
Elles s'enveloppèrent dans leurs sourires

Bonne journée j'ai vu mes amis sans soucis
Les hommes ne pesaient pas lourd
Un qui passait
Son ombre changée en souris
Fuyait dans le ruisseau

J'ai vu le ciel très grand
Le beau regard des gens privés de tout
Plage distante où personne n'aborde

Bonne journée qui commença mélancolique
Noire sous les arbres verts
Mais qui soudain trempée d'aurore
M'entra dans le cœur par surprise.

II

Montrez-moi cet homme de toujours si doux
Qui disait les doigts font monter la terre
L'arc-en-ciel qui se noue le serpent qui roule

No one can know you
Better than I know you.

⊙

TO PABLO PICASSO

I

What a fine day when I saw again the man I can't
　　forget
Whom I shall never forget
And fleeting women whose eyes
Made me a hedge of honor
Wrapped themselves in their smiles

What a fine day when I saw my carefree friends
The men did not weigh much
One who passed
His shadow changed into a mouse
Fled into the gutter

I saw a great wide sky
The magnificent looks of men deprived of
　　everything
A distant beach approached by no one

What a fine day a day begun in melancholy
Black beneath green trees
But which steeped suddenly in dawn
Entered my heart by surprise.

II

Show me this eternal man always so gentle
Who said fingers make the earth rise higher
The knotted rainbow the coiling serpent

Le miroir de chair où perle un enfant
Et ces mains tranquilles qui vont leur chemin
Nues obéissantes réduisant l'espace
Chargées de désirs et d'images
L'une suivant l'autre aiguilles de la même horloge

Montrez-moi le ciel chargé de nuages
Répétant le monde enfoui sous mes paupières
Montrez-moi le ciel dans une seule étoile
Je vois bien la terre sans être ébloui
Les pierres obscures les herbes fantômes
Ces grands verres d'eau ces grands blocs d'ambre
    des paysages
Les jeux du feu et de la cendre
Les géographies solennelles des limites humaines

Montrez-moi aussi le corsage noir
Les cheveux tirés les yeux perdus
De ces filles noires et pures qui sont d'ici de passage
    et d'ailleurs à mon gré
Qui sont de fières portes dans les murs de cet été
D'étranges jarres sans liquide toutes en vertus
Inutilement faites pour des rapports simples
Montrez-moi ces secrets qui unissent leurs tempes
A ces palais absents qui font monter la terre.

⊙

LES YEUX STERILES

Elle est comme un bourgeon
L'espace de la flamme
Candide elle a l'arome
D'amoureux enlacés.

30

[1936-1937]

Mirror of flesh in which a child is pearled
And these peaceful hands which go their way
Naked obedient reducing space
Charged with desires and images
One following the other hands of the same clock

Show me the sky laden with clouds
Repeating the world hidden beneath my eyelids
And show me the sky in a single star
I see the earth without being dazzled
The obscure stones and phantom grass
These great cups of water these mighty amber
    blocks of landscapes
The play of fire and ashes
The solemn geography of human limits

Show me as well the black corsage
The drawn hair the lost eyes
Of these black pure maidens here in passing and
    elsewhere at my will
Who are proud doors in the walls of this summer
Strange jars without liquid all in virtue
Uselessly made for simple affinities
Show me these secrets which unite their temples
To these absent palaces which make the earth rise
    higher.

⊙

THE STERILE EYES

She is like a blossom
The space of flame
Candid she has the scent
Of lovers entwined.

31

BELLE MAIN

Ce soleil qui gémit dans mon passé
N'a pas franchi le seuil
De ma main de tes mains campagne
Où renaissaient toujours
L'herbe les fleurs des promenades
Les yeux toutes leurs heures
On s'est promis des paradis et des tempêtes
Notre image a gardé nos songes

Ce soleil qui supporte la jeunesse ancienne
Ne vieillit pas il est intolérable
Il me masque l'azur profond comme un tombeau
Qu'il me faut inventer
Passionnément
Avec des mots.

⊙

SANS AGE

Nous approchons
Dans les forêts
Prenez la rue du matin
Montez les marches de la brume

Nous approchons
La terre en a le cœur crispé

Encore un jour à mettre au monde.

32

BEAUTIFUL HAND

This sun moaning in my past
Has not crossed the threshold
From my hand to your hands country
Where always were reborn
The grass the flowers of promenades
The eyes and all their hours
We promised ourselves paradise and tempests
Our image has kept our dreams

This sun which supports former youth
Does not grow old it is intolerable
It hides from me the sky deep as a tomb
Which I must invent
Passionately
With words.

⊙

AGELESS

We approach
In the forests
Take the street of morning
Mount the steps of mist

We approach
The earth's heart is shrivelled

Once more a day to put into the world.

Le ciel s'élargira
Nous en avions assez
D'habiter dans les ruines du sommeil
Dans l'ombre basse du repos
De la fatigue de l'abandon

La terre reprendra la forme de nos corps vivants
Le vent nous subira
Le soleil et la nuit passeront dans nos yeux
Sans jamais les changer

Notre espace certain notre air pur est de taille
A combler le retard creusé par l'habitude
Nous aborderons tous une mémoire nouvelle
Nous parlerons ensemble un langage sensible.

O mes frères contraires gardant dans vos prunelles
La nuit infuse et son horreur
Où vous ai-je laissés
Avec vos lourdes mains dans l'huile paresseuse
De vos actes anciens
Avec si peu d'espoir que la mort a raison
O mes frères perdus
Moi je vais vers la vie j'ai l'apparence d'homme
Pour prouver que le monde est fait à ma mesure

Et je ne suis pas seul
Mille images de moi multiplient ma lumière
Mille regards pareils égalisent la chair
C'est l'oiseau c'est l'enfant c'est le roc c'est la plaine
Qui se mêlent à nous
L'or éclate de rire de se voir hors du gouffre
L'eau le feu se dénudent pour une seule saison
Il n'y a plus d'éclipse au front de l'univers.

The sky will grow wider
We have had enough
Of living in sleep's ruins
In the low shadow of repose
Of weariness and abandon

Again the earth will take the shape of our living
　　bodies
The wind will suffer us
Sunlight and night will pass within our eyes
Without ever changing them

Our certain space our pure air is large enough
To fill the delay dug by habit
We shall all board a new memory
Together we shall speak a sensitive language.

O my contrary brothers keeping in your eyes
The infused night and its horror
Where I have left you
With your heavy hands in the idle oil
Of your past acts
With so little hope that death is right
O my lost brothers
I go towards life I have the look of a man
To prove the world is made to my measure

And I am not alone
A thousand images of me multiply my light
A thousand like glances equalize the flesh
It is the bird the child the rock the plain
Mingling with us
Gold laughs to see itself out of the chasm
Water and fire strip for a single season
There is no more eclipse on the forehead of the
　　universe.

Mains par nos mains reconnues
Lèvres à nos lèvres confondues
Les premières chaleurs florales
Alliées à la fraîcheur du sang
Le prisme respire avec nous
Aube abondante
Au sommet de chaque herbe reine
Au sommet des mousses à la pointe des neiges
Des vagues des sables bouleversés
Des enfances persistantes
Hors de toutes les cavernes
Hors de nous-mêmes.

☉

PAROLES PEINTES

à Pablo Picasso

Pour tout comprendre
Même
L'arbre au regard de proue
L'arbre adoré des lézards et des lianes
Même le feu même l'aveugle

Pour réunir aile et rosée
Cœur et nuage jour et nuit
Fenêtre et pays de partout

Pour abolir
La grimace du zéro
Qui demain roulera sur l'or

[1938]

Hands by our hands recognized
Lips to our lips melted
The first floral warmth
Bound to the coolness of the blood
The prism breathes with us
Abundant dawn
On the summit of each blade of grass queen
On the summit of moss at the tip of snow
Of waves of upset sands
Of persistent childhoods
Out of all caverns
Out of ourselves.

⊙

PAINTED WORDS

to Pablo Picasso

To understand all
Even
The tree with the look of a prow
The tree adored by vines and lizards
Even the fire even the blind man

To unite wing and dew
Heart and cloud day and night
Window and land of everywhere

To abolish
The grimace of zero
Which shall roll on gold tomorrow

Pour trancher
Les petites manières
Des géants nourris d'eux-mêmes

Pour voir tous les yeux réfléchis
Par tous les yeux

Pour voir tous les yeux aussi beaux
Que ce qu'ils voient
Mer absorbante

Pour que l'on rie légèrement
D'avoir eu chaud d'avoir eu froid
D'avoir eu faim d'avoir eu soif

Pour que parler
Soit aussi généreux
Qu'embrasser

Pour mêler baigneuse et rivière
Cristal et danseuse d'orage
Aurore et la saison des seins
Désirs et sagesse d'enfance

Pour donner à la femme
Méditative et seule
La forme des caresses
Qu'elle a rêvées

Pour que les déserts soient dans l'ombre
Au lieu d'être dans
Mon
Ombre

Donner
Mon
Bien

Donner
Mon
Droit.

To cut
The petty manners
Of giants nourished on themselves

To see all eyes reflected
By all eyes

To see all eyes as beautiful
As what they see
Absorbing ocean

So that we may laugh lightly
At having been hot at having been cold
At having been hungry at having been thirsty   ,

So that speaking
May be as generous
As kissing

To merge bather and river
Crystal and storm-dancer
Dawn and the season of the breasts
Desires and wisdom of childhood

To give to woman
Meditative and alone
The form of caresses
Of which she has dreamed

So that deserts may be in the shadow
Instead of being in
My
Shadow

To give
My
Good

To give
My
Right.

NOUS SOMMES

Tu vois le feu du soir qui sort de sa coquille
Et tu vois la forêt enfouie dans la fraîcheur

Tu vois la plaine nue aux flancs du ciel traînard
La neige haute comme la mer
Et la mer haute dans l'azur

Pierres parfaites et bois doux secours voilés
Tu vois des villes teintes de mélancolie
Dorée des trottoirs pleins d'excuses
Une place où la solitude a sa statue
Souriante et l'amour une seule maison

Tu vois les animaux
Sosies malins sacrifiés l'un à l'autre
Frères immaculés aux ombres confondues
Dans un désert de sang

Tu vois un bel enfant quand il joue quand il rit
Il est bien plus petit
Que le petit oiseau du bout des branches

Tu vois un paysage aux saveurs d'huile et d'eau
D'où la roche est exclue où la terre abandonne
Sa verdure à l'été qui la couvre de fruits

Des femmes descendant de leur miroir ancien
T'apportent leur jeunesse et leur foi en la tienne
Et l'une sa clarté la voile qui t'entraîne
Te fait secrètement voir le monde sans toi.

C'est avec nous que tout vivra

40

WE ARE

You see the fire of evening leaving its shell
And you see the forest hidden in coolness

You see the naked plain bosomed on a straggling
    sky
The snow high as the sea
And the sea high in the sky

Perfect stones and soft woods veiled assistances
You see the cities tinged with melancholy
Gilded with sidewalks full of excuses
A square where solitude has its smiling statue
And love a single house

You see the animals
Cunning counterparts sacrificed one to the other
Immaculate brothers with confused shadows
In a wilderness of blood

You see a lovely child when he plays when he
    laughs
He is much smaller
Than the small bird at the tip of the branch

You see a countryside flavored with oil and water
Where the rock is excluded where earth abandons
Her green to summer which covers her with fruit

Women descending from their ancient mirror
Bring you their youth their faith in your own
And one of them her clarity the sail which speeds
    you
Shows you secretly the world without you.

It is with us that all will live

Bêtes mes vrais étendards d'or
Plaines mes bonnes aventures
Verdure utile villes sensibles
A votre tête viendront des hommes

Des hommes de dessous les sueurs les coups les
    larmes
Mais qui vont cueillir tous leurs songes

Je vois des hommes vrais sensibles bons utiles
Rejeter un fardeau plus mince que la mort
Et dormir de joie au bruit du soleil.

☉

MEDIEUSES

I

Elle va s'éveiller d'un rêve noir et bleu
Elle va se lever de la nuit grise et mauve
Sa jambe est lisse et son pied nu
L'audace fait son premier pas

Au son d'un chant prémédité
Tout son corps passe en reflets en éclats
Son corps pavé de pluie armé de parfums tendres
Démêle le fuseau matinal de sa vie.

Animals my true gold standards
Plains my good adventures
Useful grass sensitive cities
Men will come to your head

Men from below the sweats the blows the tears
But who will pluck all their dreams

I see true men good sensitive useful
Cast down a burden thinner than death
And sleep with joy in the sound of sunlight.

⊙

MEDIEUSES

I

She is going to waken from a blue black dream
She is going to rise from the grey and purple night
Her leg is smooth her foot naked
Audacity takes its first step

At the sound of a premeditated song
All of her body passes in reflections in brilliance
Her body paved with rain armed with tender
      perfumes
Unwinds the morning distaff of her life.

II

Près de l'aigrette du grand pont
L'orgueil au large
J'attends tout ce que j'ai connu
Comblée d'espace scintillant
Ma mémoire est immense

La bonté danse sur mes lèvres
Des haillons tièdes m'illuminent
Une route part de mon front

Proche et lointaine
La mer bondit et me salue
Elle a la forme d'une grappe
D'un plaisir mûr

J'aimais hier et j'aime encore
Je ne me dérobe à rien
Mon passé m'est fidèle
Le temps court dans mes veines.

III

Sous des poutres usées sous des plafonds stériles
Dans une vaste chambre petitement garnie
Les genoux ligotés confèrent qualité
A la ligne droite misérable

Ses cheveux pris au piège d'un miroir brisé
C'est sur la mousse de son front que l'eau roucoule
La dérive évasive d'un sourire entraîne
Sa dernière illusion vers un ciel disparu.

[1939]

II

Near the crest of the great bridge
Pride far at sea
I await all I have known
Filled with shining space
My memory is immense

Goodness dances on my lips
Warm rags illuminate me
A road leaves my forehead

Near and far
The sea leaps and does me homage
It has the form of a cluster
Of ripe pleasure

Yesterday I loved and still I love
I avoid nothing
My past is faithful to me
Time runs in my veins.

III

Beneath worn beams beneath sterile ceilings
In a vast chamber slightly furnished
The bound knees confer quality
On the miserable straight line

Her hair caught in the trap of a broken mirror
Water warbles on the moss of her forehead
The evasive drift of a smile draws
Her last illusion toward a vanished sky.

45

IV

Dans les parages de son lit rampe la terre
Et les bêtes de la terre et les hommes de la terre
Dans les parages de son lit
Il n'y a que des champs de blé
Vignes et champs de pensées
La route est tracée sans outils
Les mains les yeux mènent au lit
A l'ardent secret révélé
Aux ombres taillées en songe

Délié des doigts de l'air l'élan
Le vase d'or d'un baiser

La gorge lourde et lente
Par mille gerbes balancée
Arrive aux fêtes de ses fleurs

Elle donne soif et faim

Son corps est un amoureux nu
Il s'échappe de ses yeux
Et la lumière noue la nuit la chair la terre
La lumière sans fond d'un corps abandonné
Et de deux yeux qui se répètent.

V

Mes sœurs prennent dans leurs toiles
Les cris et les plaintes des chiens
Moi je préfère me nourrir
De l'espoir d'une ardeur sans fin
Oranger noir armure blonde
Grisante abeille rire en course

46

[1939]

IV

The earth creeps in the latitudes of her bed
The beasts of the earth and the men of the earth
In the latitudes of her bed
There are only wheatfields
Vineyards and fields of pansies
The road is traced without tools
The hands the eyes lead to the bed
To the ardent secret revealed
To shadows fashioned in dream

Unbound by the fingers of the air the surge
The golden vase of a kiss

The throat slow and heavy
Balanced by a thousand sheaves
Arrives at her festivals of flowers

She gives thirst and hunger

Her body is a naked lover
It escapes from her eyes
And light knots night and flesh and earth
The depthless light of an abandoned body
And of two eyes which repeat themselves.

V

My sisters take in their webs
The cries and whimpers of dogs
But I prefer to feed myself
On the hope of an endless ardor
Black orange-tree fair armor
Reeling bee racing laughter

Rire invisiblement masqué
Ecorce d'aube aile étourdie
Nichée de feuilles débauchées
Jeune poison liane montagne
Sueur de nage fumée froide
Pas de géant danse battante
Front éternel paume parfaite
Puits en plein air essieu de vent
Monument vague flamant fou
Jeu sans perdant santé sans trous
Torche brûlant dans l'eau tour mixte
Martyr radieux aux angles vifs
Œil clair à travers honte et brume
Première neige réjouissante
Mérite de la solitude
Exil aux sources de la force.

VI

Où es-tu me vois-tu m'entends-tu
Me reconnaîtras-tu
Moi la plus belle la seule
Je tiens le flot de la rivière comme un violon
Je laisse passer les jours
Je laisse passer les bateaux les nuages
L'ennui est mort près de moi
Je tiens tous les échos d'enfance mes trésors
Avec des rires dans mon cou

Mon paysage est un bien grand bonheur
Et mon visage un limpide univers
Ailleurs on pleure des larmes noires
On va de caverne en caverne
Ici on ne peut pas se perdre

Laughter invisibly masked
Bark of dawn heedless wing
Brood of debauched leaves
Young poison mountain vine
Sweat of swimming cold smoke
Giant step beating dance
Eternal forehead perfect palm
Wells in open air axle of wind
Vague monument flaming mad
Game without losers health without holes
Torch burning in the water mixed turn
Radiant martyr with live angles
Clear eye through shame and mist
First rejoicing snow
Merit of solitude
Exile to the springs of strength.

VI

Where are you do you see me do you hear me
Will you recognize me
I the loveliest I alone
I hold the tide of the river like a violin
I let the days pass
I let boats and clouds pass
Weariness is dead beside me
I hold all the echoes of childhood my treasures
With laughter in my throat

My landscape is a very great happiness
And my face a limpid universe
Elsewhere they weep black tears
They go from cavern to cavern
Here you cannot lose yourself

Et mon visage est dans l'eau pure je le vois
Chanter un seul arbre
Adoucir des cailloux
Refléter l'horizon
Je m'appuie contre l'arbre
Couche sur les cailloux
Sur l'eau j'applaudis le soleil la pluie
Et le vent sérieux

Où es-tu me vois-tu m'entends-tu
Je suis la créature de derrière le rideau
De derrière le premier rideau venu
Maîtresse des verdures malgré tout
Et des plantes de rien
Maîtresse de l'eau maîtresse de l'air
Je domine ma solitude
Où es-tu
A force de rêver de moi le long des murs
Tu me vois tu m'entends
Et tu voudrais changer mon cœur
M'arracher au sein de mes yeux

J'ai le pouvoir d'exister sans destin
Entre givre et rosée entre oubli et présence

Fraîcheur chaleur je n'en ai pas souci
Je ferai s'éloigner à travers tes désirs
L'image de moi-même que tu m'offres

Mon visage n'a qu'une étoile

Il faut céder m'aimer en vain
Je suis éclipse rêve de nuit
Oublie mes rideaux de cristal

And my face is in the pure water I see it
Sing a single tree
Soften stones
Reflect the horizon
I lean against the tree
Sleep on stones
On water I applaud the sun the rain
And the serious wind

Where are you do you see me do you hear me
I am the creature behind the curtain
Behind the first curtain to come
Mistress of green grass in spite of all
And plants of nothing
Mistress of water mistress of air
I dominate my solitude
Where are you
Because you dream of me along the walls
You see and hear me
And you would change my heart
Tear me from the depths of my eyes

I have the power to exist without destiny
Between frost and dew between oblivion and
    presence

Coolness and warmth I care nothing for them
I shall send far across your desires
The image of myself you offer me

My face has but one star

You must yield to loving me in vain
I am eclipse and dream of night
Forget my crystal curtains

51

Je reste dans mes propres feuilles
Je reste mon propre miroir
Je mêle la neige et le feu
Mes cailloux ont ma douceur
Ma saison est éternelle.

VII

Et par la grâce de ta lèvre arme la mienne.

⊙

VIVRE

Nous avons tous deux nos mains à donner
Prenez ma main je vous conduirai loin

J'ai vécu plusieurs fois mon visage a changé
A chaque seuil à chaque main que j'ai franchis
Le printemps familial renaissait

Gardant pour lui pour moi sa neige périssable
La mort et la promise
La future aux cinq doigts serrés et relâchés

Mon âge m'accordait toujours
De nouvelles raisons de vivre par autrui
Et d'avoir en mon cœur le sang d'un autre cœur

Ah le garçon lucide que je fus et que je suis
Devant la blancheur des faibles filles aveugles
Plus belles que la lune blonde fine usée
Par le reflet des chemins de la vie

I remain in my own leaves
I remain my own mirror
I mingle snow and fire
My pebbles have my sweetness
My season is eternal.

VII

And by the grace of your lips arm mine.

⊙

TO LIVE

We both have our hands to give
Take mine and I shall lead you far

I have lived several times my face has changed
At each threshold at each hand that I have crossed
The family springtime was reborn

Keeping for it for me its perishable snow
Death and the betrothed
The future with five fingers clenched and relaxed

Always my age accorded me
New reasons for living by others
For having in my heart the blood of another heart

Ah the lucid boy I used to be and that I am
Before the whiteness of frail blind girls
More lovely than the fair fine moon worn out
By the reflection of the roads of life

53

Chemin des mousses et des arbres
Du brouillard et de la rosée
Du jeune corps qui ne monte pas seul
A sa place sur terre
Le vent le froid la pluie le bercent
L'été en fait un homme

Présence ma vertu dans chaque main visible
La seule mort c'est solitude
De délice en furie de furie en clarté
Je me construis entier à travers tous les êtres
A travers tous les temps au sol et dans les nues
Saisons passantes je suis jeune
Et fort à force d'avoir vécu
Je suis jeune et mon sang s'élève sur mes ruines

Nous avons nos mains à mêler
Rien jamais ne peut mieux séduire
Que notre attachement l'un à l'autre forêt
Rendant la terre au ciel et le ciel à la nuit

A la nuit qui prépare un jour interminable.

⊙

FINIR

Les pieds dans des souliers d'or fin
Les jambes dans l'argile froide
Debout les murs couverts de viandes inutiles
Debout les bêtes mortes
Voici qu'un tourbillon gluant
Fixe à jamais rides grimaces

54

Roads of moss and trees
Of mist and dew
Of a young body which does not rise alone
To its place on earth
The wind the cold and rain cradle it
Summer makes a man of it

Presence my virtue in each visible hand
The only death is solitude
From delight to fury from fury to clarity
I build myself completely through all beings
Through all times in the earth and in the clouds
Passing seasons I am young
Strong in the strength of having lived
I am young and my blood rises above my ruins

We have our hands to entwine
Nothing can ever seduce better
Than our attachment one to the other forest
Giving earth back to sky and sky to night

To night which prepares an endless day.

⊙

TO FINISH

Feet in the shoes of fine gold
Legs in cold clay
Standing the walls covered with useless flesh
Standing the dead beasts
Here a glutinous whirlwind
Fixes forever wrinkles grimaces

Voici que les cercueils enfantent
Que les verres sont pleins de sable
Et vides
Voici que les noyés s'enfoncent
Le sang détruit
Dans l'eau sans fond de leurs espoirs passés

Feuille morte molle rancœur
Contre le désir et la joie
Le repos a trouvé son maître
Sur des lits de pierre et d'épines

La charrue des mots est rouillée
Aucun sillon d'amour n'aborde plus la chair
Un lugubre travail est jeté en pâture
A la misère dévorante
A bas les murs couverts des armes émouvantes
Qui voyaient clair dans l'homme
Des hommes noircissent de honte
D'autres célèbrent leur ordure
Les yeux les meilleurs s'abandonnent

Même les chiens sont malheureux.

☉

RENCONTRES

à Germaine et Georges Hugnet

I

Doux monstre tu tiens la mort dans ton bec
Doux monstre à tes seins perle le bon lait
Dans tes yeux heureux mes yeux malheureux

[1940]

Here coffins give birth
And glasses are full of sand
And empty
Here drowned men sink
Their blood destroyed
In the depthless water of their past hopes

Dead leaf soft rancor
Against desire and joy
Repose has found its master
On a bed of stones and thorns

The plow of words is rusted
Furrows of love no longer approach the flesh
A dismal work is thrown into pasture
To devouring misery
Down with walls covered with alarming weapons
Which saw clearly in man
Men blacken with shame
Others celebrate their offal
The best eyes are abandoned

Even the dogs are unhappy.

⊙

MEETINGS

to Germaine and Georges Hugnet

I

Sweet monster you hold death in your beak
Sweet monster the good milk pearls at your breasts
In your happy eyes my wretched eyes

Vont faucher le blé tarir les fontaines
Détourner de toi les routes humaines.

II

Les ours cruels et ravissants
Nés le jour même de la guerre
Prononcent des vœux innocents.

III

La cellule du prisonnier
Qui n'était pas trop grande pour une araignée.

IV

Orvet fléau de la balance
Entre deux haines transparentes.

V

Attention tes plumes débordent
Tu trembles de ne pas voler.

VI

Me voici né quelle erreur
Dit l'ami chien pour toujours.

VII

Les champs roses verts et jaunes
Sont des insectes éclatants
Partis
De mon infini champ de mai.

[1940]

Go to cut the wheat dry up the fountains
And turn the human roads away from you.

II

The cruel ravishing bears
Born the same day as the war
Pronounce innocent wishes.

III

The prisoner's cell
Which was not too large for a spider.

IV

Blindworm beam of the balance
Between two transparent hatreds.

V

Look out your feathers overflow
You tremble at not flying.

VI

Here I am born what a mistake
Says friend dog for always.

VII

The fields pink green yellow
Are brilliant insects
Gone
From my infinite field of May.

VIII

Maisons et rues éteintes en mes oreilles
Je rêve de vous corbeaux qui chantez le silence

Corbeaux le bec enfariné
Si vieux
Qu'ils ne se savent plus au monde.

IX

Ici mille pies contrarient
Mille petites lunes diurnes.

X

Pour nous faire oublier le froid
Sur la neige un doigt dessina
La silhouette blonde d'un lion.

XI

Prenez garde à vos pattes
L'homme a les pieds en sang.

☉

PATIENCE

Toi ma patiente ma patience ma parente
Gorge haut suspendue orgue de la nuit lente
Révérence cachant tous les ciels dans sa grâce
Prépare à la vengeance un lit d'où je naîtrai.

VIII

Houses and streets extinguished in my ears
I dream of you crows who sing the silence

Crows with encrusted beaks
So old
That they know themselves no longer in the world.

IX

Here a thousand magpies dispute
A thousand little diurnal moons.

X

To make us forget the cold
On the snow a finger traced
The blonde silhouette of a lion.

XI

Be careful of your paws
Man has his feet in blood.

⊙

PATIENCE

You my patient woman my patience my parent
Throat high suspended organ of slow night
Reverence hiding all skies in its grace
Prepare for vengeance a bed from which I shall be
    born.

LE DROIT LE DEVOIR DE VIVRE

Il n'y aurait rien
Pas un insecte bourdonnant
Pas une feuille frissonnante
Pas un animal léchant ou hurlant
Rien de chaud rien de fleuri
Rien de givré rien de brillant rien d'odorant
Pas une ombre léchée par la fleur de l'été
Pas un arbre portant des fourrures de neige
Pas une joue fardée par un baiser joyeux
Pas une aile prudente‚ ou hardie dans le vent
Pas un coin de chair fine pas un bras chantant
Rien de libre ni de gagner ni de gâcher
Ni de s'éparpiller ni de se réunir
Pour le bien pour le mal
Pas une nuit armée d'amour ou de repos
Pas une voix d'aplomb pas une bouche émue
Pas un sein dévoilé pas une main ouverte
Pas de misère et pas de satiété
Rien d'opaque rien de visible
Rien de lourd rien de léger
Rien de mortel rien d'éternel

Il y aurait un homme
N'importe quel homme
Moi ou un autre
Sinon il n'y aurait rien.

[1941]

THE RIGHT THE DUTY TO LIVE

There would be nothing
Not a buzzing insect
Not a trembling leaf
Not an animal licking or howling
Nothing warm nothing flowering
Nothing frosted nothing brilliant nothing odorous
Not a shadow licked by the flower of summer
Not a tree wearing the fur-piece of snow
Not a cheek painted by a joyous kiss
Not a wing prudent or bold in the wind
Not a corner of delicate flesh not a singing arm
Nothing free nothing to win nor spoil
Nor scatter nor unite again
For good for evil
Not a night armed in love or rest
Not a voice of assurance not a fervid mouth
Not an unveiled breast not an open hand
No misery and no satiety
Nothing opaque nothing visible
Nothing heavy nothing light
Nothing mortal nothing eternal

There would be a man
No matter what man
Myself or another
If not there would be nothing.

LE MONDE EST NUL

I

Fausses guenons et fausses araignées
Fausses taupes et fausses truies
Et parfois l'ombre d'une biche
Sauvagement bêtes et malheureuses
Timidement femmes illuminées

Ensevelies secouant leur linceul
Femmes de craie femmes de suie
Brûlées le jour d'un feu nocturne
Glacées la nuit par un monstre visible
Leur propre image éternellement seule

Chantant la mort sur les airs de la vie
La terre leur est familière
Terre sans graines sans racines
Sans la lumière agile du dehors
Sans les clés d'or de l'espace interdit.

II

Petite et belle elle peut vivre sans miroir
Petite et belle elle peut vivre sans espoir

Les longs charrois de nuit et l'aube à petit feu
Ont dégradé son corps ont dévasté son cœur

Vivre toujours peut-être et patient je regarde
Le jour pâle épouser sans plaisir ses yeux vagues.

[1942]

THE WORLD IS NIL

I

False apes and false spiders
False moles and false sows
And sometimes the shadow of a doe
Savagely stupid and unhappy
Timidly women illuminated

Entombed shaking their shrouds
Women of chalk women of soot
Burned by day in a nocturnal fire
Frozen at night by a visible monster
Their own image eternally alone

Singing death to the tunes of life
The earth is familiar to them
Seedless rootless earth
Without the agile light of the outside
Without the golden keys of forbidden space.

II

Small and beautiful she can live without a mirror
Small and beautiful she can live without hope

The long carriages of night and the simmering
dawn
Have degraded her body laid her heart to waste

To live perhaps forever and patient I regard
The pale day wed without pleasure her vague eyes.

III

Le visage pourri par des flots de tristesse
Comme un bois très précieux dans la forêt épaisse
Elle donnait aux rats la fin de sa vieillesse
Ses doigts leur égrenaient gâteries et caresses

Elle ne parlait plus elle ne mangeait plus.

IV

Impérieusement elle ordonnait aux hommes
De se mettre à l'abri sous de bonnes ordures
Elle hurlait je suis la putain du Seigneur
Une fille de rien je sors de la nuit noire
Par une étoile dérobée
Et je commande avec une langue de boue
Que l'on m'aime à jamais.

V

Ecrasée accablée appliquée à vieillir
Et mes sœurs me devaient quinze millions de
    siècles
La cadette voyait plus clair à travers moi
Qu'à travers l'Algérie trapue un continent
Moulé pétri laqué par des chaleurs d'argent

J'arborais un enfant sur mon sein transparent
Dans un berceau de verre un tonnerre d'enfant
Régnant sans le secours de la mort ni du ciel
Les oiseaux souvolaient les monts et les vallées
Les poissons s'en allaient de tous les océans.

III

Her face rotted by floods of sadness
Like very precious wood in the thick forest
She gave the end of her old age to the rats
Her fingers shelled them indulgences and caresses

She spoke no more she ate no more.

IV

Imperiously she ordered men
To shield themselves beneath good offal
She screamed I am the whore of God
A good for nothing I spring from the black night
By a stolen star
And I command with a tongue of mud
That I be loved forever.

V

Crushed overwhelmed determined to grow old
And my sisters owed me fifteen million centuries
The younger one saw more clearly through me
Than through squat Algeria a continent
Moulded kneaded lacquered by the silver heat

I planted a child on my transparent breast
In a cradle of glass a thunder of a child
Reigning without help of death or heaven
Birds flew below the mountains and valleys
Fish deserted all oceans.

VI

Qui suis-je et ce marron et son sucre intérieur
Ce mannequin en croix est-il un homme ou moi
Vous parlez par ma voix vous m'avez déchaînée
Et moi je vous enchaîne sans savoir pourquoi.

VII

J'ai pour la foudre chue un respect de vaincue
Mes os sont calcinés ma couronne est brisée
Je pleure et l'on en rit ma souffrance est souillée
Et le mur du regret cerne mon existence
Peut-être aurais-je pu me masquer de beauté
Peut-être aurais-je pu cacher cette innocence
Qui fait peur aux enfants.

Sainte-Anne, 1942.

⊙

AVIS

La nuit qui précéda sa mort
Fut la plus courte de sa vie
L'idée qu'il existait encore
Lui brûlait le sang aux poignets
Le poids de son corps l'écœurait
Sa force le faisait gémir
C'est tout au fond de cette horreur
Qu'il a commencé à sourire
Il n'avait pas *un* camarade.
Mais des millions et des millions
Pour le venger il le savait
Et le jour se leva pour lui.

VI

Who am I both this chestnut and its inner sugar
This mannequin on the cross is he a man or me
You speak with my voice you have unchained me
And I enchain you without knowing why.

VII

For fallen lightning I have the respect of the
    conquered
My bones have turned to chalk my crown is broken
I weep they laugh at it my suffering is soiled
And the wall of regret circles my existence
Perhaps I could have masked myself in beauty
Perhaps I could have hidden this innocence
Which frightens children.

Sainte-Anne, 1942.

☉

NOTICE

The night before his death
Was the shortest of his life
The idea that he still existed
Burned the blood in his wrists
The weight of his body sickened him
His strength made him groan
It was at the very bottom of this horror
That he began to smile
He had not *one* comrade
But millions and millions
To avenge him and he knew it
And the sun rose for him.

COURAGE

Paris a froid Paris a faim
Paris ne mange plus de marrons dans la rue
Paris a mis de vieux vêtements de vieille
Paris dort tout debout sans air dans le métro
Plus de malheur encore est imposé aux pauvres
Et la sagesse et la folie
De Paris malheureux
C'est l'air pur c'est le feu
C'est la beauté c'est la bonté
De ses travailleurs affamés
Ne crie pas au secours Paris
Tu es vivant d'une vie sans égale
Et derrière la nudité
De ta pâleur de ta maigreur
Tout ce qui est humain se révèle en tes yeux
Paris ma belle ville
Fine comme une aiguille forte comme une épée
Ingénue et savante
Tu ne supportes pas l'injustice
Pour toi c'est le seul désordre
Tu vas te libérer Paris
Paris tremblant comme une étoile
Notre espoir survivant
Tu vas te libérer de la fatigue et de la boue
Frères ayons du courage
Nous qui ne sommes pas casqués
Ni bottés ni gantés ni bien élevés
Un rayon s'allume en nos veines
Notre lumière nous revient
Les meilleurs d'entre nous sont morts pour nous
Et voici que leur sang retrouve notre cœur
Et c'est de nouveau le matin un matin de Paris
La pointe de la délivrance
L'espace du printemps naissant
La force idiote a le dessous

COURAGE

Paris is cold Paris is hungry
Paris no longer eats chestnuts in the street
Paris has put on the old clothes of an old woman
Paris sleeps standing in the airless métro
Still more suffering is imposed on the poor
And the wisdom and the folly
Of unhappy Paris
Is the pure air the fire
The beauty the goodness
Of her famished workers
Do not cry help Paris
You are living a life without equal
And behind the nakedness
Of your pallor of your lean bodies
All that is human is revealed in your eyes
Paris my lovely city
Fine as a needle strong as a sword
Simple and knowing
You tolerate no injustice
For you it is the sole disorder
You shall free yourself Paris
Paris trembling as a star
Our hope surviving
You shall free yourself from weariness and mire
Brothers let us have courage
We who wear no helmet
Neither shod nor gloved nor well brought up
A ray of light shines in our veins
Our light comes back to us
The best of us have died for us
Now their blood finds our heart again
And once again it is morning a Paris morning
The point of deliverance
The space of a nascent springtime
Idiot force has the worst of it

Ces esclaves nos ennemis
S'ils ont compris
S'ils sont capables de comprendre
Vont se lever.

⊙

CHANT NAZI

Le voi fou d'un papillon
La fenêtre l'évasion
Le soleil interminable
La promesse inépuisable
Et qui se joue bien des balles
Cerne les yeux d'un frisson

L'arbre est neuf l'arbre est saignant
Mes enfants c'est le printemps
La dernière des saisons
Hâtez-vous profitez-en
C'est le bagne ou la prison
La fusillade ou le front

Dernière fête des mères
Le cœur cède saluons
Partout la mort la misère
Et l'Allemagne asservie
Et l'Allemagne accroupie
Dans le sang et la sanie
Dans les plaies qu'elle a creusées
Notre tâche est terminée

Ainsi chantent chantent bien
Les bons maîtres assassins.

72

[1944]

These slaves our enemies
If they have understood
If they are able to understand
Will rise.

⊙

NAZI SONG

The mad flight of a butterfly
The window the escape
The interminable sun
The inexhaustible promise
Which makes sport of bullets
Circles the eyes with a shudder

The tree is new the tree is bleeding
My children it is springtime
The last of the seasons
Hasten and enjoy it
It is the death-camp or the prison
The rifle-shot or the front

This is the last mothers' festival
The heart surrenders let us do homage
Everywhere to death and misery
And Germany enslaved
And Germany cowering
In the blood in the pus
In the open wounds she has dug
Our task is finished

So sing and sing well
The good master assassins.

LES SEPT POEMES D'AMOUR EN GUERRE

« J'écris dans ce pays où l'on parque les hommes
Dans l'ordure et la soif le silence et la faim... »

ARAGON (*Le Musée Grévin*).

I

Un navire dans tes yeux
Se rendait maître du vent
Tes yeux étaient le pays
Que l'on retrouve en un instant

Patients tes yeux nous attendaient

Sous les arbres des forêts
Dans la pluie dans la tourmente
Sur la neige des sommets
Entre les yeux et les jeux des enfants

Patients tes yeux nous attendaient

Ils étaient une vallée
Plus tendre qu'un seul brin d'herbe
Leur soleil donnait du poids
Aux maigres moissons humaines

Nous attendaient pour nous voir
Toujours
Car nous apportions l'amour
La jeunesse de l'amour
Et la raison de l'amour
La sagesse de l'amour
Et l'immortalité.

74

[1943]

SEVEN POEMS OF LOVE IN WAR

« *I am writing in this land where they pen up men
In offal and thirst, silence and starvation...* »

ARAGON (*Le Musée Grévin*).

I

A ship in your eyes
Became master of the wind
And your eyes were the country
Found again in an instant

Patient your eyes waited for us

Under the trees of the forests
In rain in torment
On the snow of mountain peaks
Among the eyes and the games of children

Patient your eyes waited for us

They were a valley
More tender than a single blade of grass
Their sunlight gave substance
To the lean human harvest

They waited to see us
Always
For we brought love
The youth of love
And the reason of love
The wisdom of love
And immortality.

75

II

Jour de nos yeux mieux peuplés
Que les plus grandes batailles

Villes et banlieues villages
De nos yeux vainqueurs du temps

Dans la fraîche vallée brûlé
Le soleil fluide et fort

Et sur l'herbe se pavane
La chair rose du printemps

Le soir a fermé ses ailes
Sur Paris désespéré
Notre lampe soutient la nuit
Comme un captif la liberté.

III

La source coulant douce et nue
La nuit partout épanouie
La nuit où nous nous unissons
Dans une lutte faible et folle

Et la nuit qui nous fait injure
La nuit où se creuse le lit
Vide de la solitude
L'avenir d'une agonie.

IV

C'est une plante qui frappe
A la porte de la terre

[1943]

II

Light of our eyes more populous
Than the greatest battles

Towns and suburbs villages
Of our eyes conquerors of time

In the cool valley the sun
Burns bright and fluid

And the rose flesh of springtime
Struts upon the grass

Evening has folded its wings
Over a Paris without hope
But our lamp sustains the night
As a captive liberty.

III

The spring flowing sweet and naked
Night stretches everywhere
The night when we join together
In a mad and feeble struggle

And the night which curses us
The night when the empty bed
Of solitude is dug
The future of an agony.

IV

A flower knocks
At the gates of the earth

Et c'est un enfant qui frappe
A la porte de sa mère
C'est la pluie et le soleil
Qui naissent avec l'enfant
Grandissent avec la plante
Fleurissent avec l'enfant

J'entends raisonner et rire.

On a calculé la peine
Qu'on peut faire à un enfant
Tant de honte sans vomir
Tant de larmes sans périr

Un bruit de pas sous la voûte
Noire et béate d'horreur
On vient déterrer la plante
On vient avilir l'enfant

Par la misère et l'ennui.

V

Le coin du cœur disaient-ils gentiment
Le coin d'amour et de haine et de gloire
Répondions-nous et nos yeux reflétaient
La vérité qui nous servait d'asile

Nous n'avons jamais commencé
Nous nous sommes toujours aimés
Et parce que nous nous aimons
Nous voulons libérer les autres
De leur solitude glacée

[1943]

A child knocks
At the door of his mother
The rain and sunlight
Born with the child
Growing with the flower
Flowering with the child

I hear reasoning and laughter.

They have calculated the sorrow
That a child can bear
So much shame without vomiting
So many tears without dying

There is a sound of footsteps under the archways
Black and blest with horror
They are coming to uproot the flower
They are coming to vilify the child

With misery and weariness.

V

The heart's corner they said softly
The corner of love and hate and glory
We answered and our eyes reflected
The truth which was our sanctuary

We have never begun
But we have always been in love
And because we are in love
We want to free others
From their icy solitude

Nous voulons et je dis je veux
Je dis tu veux et nous voulons
Que la lumière perpétue
Des couples brillants de vertu
Des couples cuirassés d'audace
Parce que leurs yeux se font face

Et qu'ils ont leur but dans la vie des autres.

VI

Nous ne vous chantons pas trompettes
Pour mieux vous montrer le malheur
Tel qu'il est très grand très bête
Et plus bête d'être entier

Nous prétendions seule la mort
Seule la terre nous limite
Mais maintenant c'est la honte
Qui nous mure tout vivants

Honte du mal illimité
Honte de nos bourreaux absurdes
Toujours les mêmes toujours
Les mêmes amants d'eux-mêmes

Honte des trains de suppliciés
Honte des mots terre brûlée
Mais nous n'avons pas honte de notre souffrance
Mais nous n'avons pas honte d'avoir honte

Derrière les guerriers fuyards
Même plus ne vit un oiseau
L'air est vide de sanglots
Vide de notre innocence

Retentissant de haine et de vengeance.

We want and I say I want
I say that you want and we want
Light to perpetuate
Couples shining with virtue
Couples armed with audacity
Because they look into each other's eyes

And their goal is in the lives of others.

VI

We do not trumpet our misfortune
The better to show you our unhappiness
Such as it is very great very stupid
And all the more stupid because it is complete

We claimed that death alone
That earth alone could limit us
But now it is shame
That walls us up alive

Shame of unbounded evil
Shame of our absurd butchers
Always the same always
The same lovers of themselves

Shame of the trainloads of the tortured
Shame of the words scorched earth
But we are not ashamed of our suffering
We are not ashamed of our shame

Not even a bird is left alive
In the wake of these coward warriors
The air is empty of sobbing
Empty of our innocence

Resounding with hate and vengeance.

VII

Au nom du front parfait profond
Au nom des yeux que je regarde
Et de la bouche que j'embrasse
Pour aujourd'hui et pour toujours

Au nom de l'espoir enterré
Au nom des larmes dans le noir
Au nom des plaintes qui font rire
Au nom des rires qui font peur

Au nom des rires dans la rue
De la douceur qui lie nos mains
Au nom des fruits couvrant les fleurs
Sur une terre belle et bonne

Au nom des hommes en prison
Au nom des femmes déportées
Au nom de tous nos camarades
Martyrisés et massacrés
Pour n'avoir pas accepté l'ombre

Il nous faut drainer la colère
Et faire se lever le fer
Pour préserver l'image haute
Des innocents partout traqués
Et qui partout vont triompher.

[1943]

VII

In the name of the perfect profound face
In the name of the eyes I look at
And the mouth I kiss
For today and for always

In the name of buried hope
In the name of tears in the darkness
In the name of sorrow that brings laughter
In the name of laughter that brings fear

In the name of laughter in the street
Of the gentleness that links our hands
In the name of fruits covering flowers
On an earth good and beautiful

In the name of the men in prison
In the name of the women deported
In the name of all our comrades
Martyred and massacred
For not accepting the shadow

We must drain our rage
And make the iron rise up
To preserve the high image
Of the innocent everywhere hunted
And who will triumph everywhere.

CRITIQUE DE LA POESIE

Le feu réveille la forêt
Les troncs les cœurs les mains les feuilles
Le bonheur en un seul bouquet
Confus léger fondant sucré
C'est toute une forêt d'amis
Qui s'assemble aux fontaines vertes
Du bon soleil du bois flambant

García Lorca a été mis à mort

Maison d'une seule parole
Et des lèvres unies pour vivre
Un tout petit enfant sans larmes
Dans ses prunelles d'eau perdue
La lumière de l'avenir
Goutte à goutte elle comble l'homme
Jusqu'aux paupières transparentes

Saint-Pol Roux a été mis à mort
Sa fille a été suppliciée

Ville glacée d'angles semblables
Où je rêve de fruits en fleur
Du ciel entier et la terre
Comme à de vierges découvertes
Dans un jeu qui n'en finit pas
Pierres fanées murs sans écho
Je vous évite d'un sourire

Decour a été mis à mort.

CRITIQUE OF POETRY

Fire wakens the forest
The trunks of trees the hearts the leaves the hands
Happiness in a single bouquet
Confused airy melting sweetened
It is a whole forest of friends
Meeting at the green fountains
In the fine sun of the flaming woods

García Lorca has been put to death

House of a single word
And of lips joined for living
A little child without tears
In his eyes of lost water
The light of the future
Drop by drop fills man
Up to his transparent eyelids

Saint-Pol Roux has been put to death
His daughter has been tortured

City iced by similar angles
Where I dream of ripening fruit
Of an integral sky and of the earth
As of virgin discoveries
In a never-ending game
Faded stones walls without echo
I avoid you with a smile

Decour has been put to death.

L'AUBE DISSOUT LES MONSTRES

Ils ignoraient
Que la beauté de l'homme est plus grande que
    l'homme

Ils vivaient pour penser ils pensaient pour se taire
Ils vivaient pour mourir ils étaient inutiles
Ils recouvraient leur innocence dans la mort

Ils avaient mis en ordre
Sous le nom de richesse
Leur misère leur bien-aimée

Ils mâchonnaient des fleurs et des sourires
Ils ne trouvaient de cœur qu'au bout de leur fusil

Ils ne comprenaient pas les injures des pauvres
Des pauvres sans soucis demain

Des rêves sans soleil les rendaient éternels
Mais pour que le nuage changeât en boue
Ils descendaient ils ne faisaient plus tête au ciel

Toute leur nuit leur mort leur belle ombre misère
Misère pour les autres

Nous oublierons ces ennemis indifférents

Une foule bientôt
Répétera la claire flamme à voix très douce
La flamme pour nous deux pour nous seuls
    patience
Pour nous deux en tout lieu le baiser des vivants.

[1943]

DAWN DISSOLVES THE MONSTERS

They did not know
That the beauty of man is greater than man

They lived to think they thought to keep silent
They lived to die and they were useless
They recovered their innocence in death

They had put in order
In the name of riches
Their misery their beloved

They gnawed away the flowers and the smiles
They found a heart only at the end of their rifles

They did not understand the curses of the poor
Of the poor carefree tomorrow

Sunless dreams made them eternal
But to change the cloud to mud
They went down they looked no longer at the sky

All their night their death their fine shadow misery
Misery for the others

We shall forget these indifferent enemies

Soon masses
Will repeat the bright flame in a very gentle voice
The flame for us two for us alone patience
For us two in every place the kiss of the living.

ENTERRAR Y CALLAR

Frères cette aurore est vôtre
Cette aurore à fleur de terre
Est votre dernière aurore
Vous vous y êtes couchés
Frères cette aurore est nôtre
Sur ce gouffre de douleur

Et par cœur et par courroux
Frères nous tenons à vous
Nous voulons éterniser
Cette aurore qui partage
Votre tombe blanche et noire
L'espoir et le désespoir

La haine sortant de terre
Et combattant pour l'amour
La haine dans la poussière
Ayant satisfait l'amour
L'amour brillant en plein jour
Toujours vit l'espoir sur terre.

⊙

LES ARMES DE LA DOULEUR

Au père :

Daddy des Ruines
Homme au chapeau troué
Homme aux orbites creuses
Homme au feu noir
Homme au ciel vide
Corbeau fait pour vivre vieux
Tu avais rêvé d'être heureux

ENTERRAR Y CALLAR

Brothers this dawn is your own
This flowering daybreak of earth
Is your last dawn
And dawn shall be your bed
Brothers this dawn is our own
Daybreak over a gulf of sorrow

And by our heart and by our anger
Brothers we stand by you
We will immortalise
This dawn which shares
Your tomb of white and black
Of hope and despair

Hate springing from the ground
And fighting for love
Hate in the dust
Having satisfied love
Love burning in broad daylight
Always sees hope on earth.

⊙

THE WEAPONS OF SORROW

To the father :

Daddy of Ruins
Man with a hole in his hat
Man with sunken eyes
Man of black fire
Man of empty sky
Crow born to live old
You dreamed of being happy

Daddy des Ruines
Ton fils est mort
Assassiné

Daddy la Haine
O victime cruelle
Mon camarade de deux guerres
Notre vie est tailladée
Saignante et laide
Mais nous jurons
De tenir bientôt le couteau

Daddy l'Espoir
L'espoir des autres
Tu es partout.

⊙

Et c'est la mère qui parle :

J'avais dans nos serments bâti trois châteaux
Un pour la vie un pour la mort un pour l'amour
    Je cachais comme un trésor
    Les pauvres petites peines
    De ma vie heureuse et bonne

J'avais dans la douceur tissé trois manteaux
Un pour nous deux et deux pour notre enfant
    Nous avions les mêmes mains
    Et nous pensions l'un pour l'autre
    Nous embellissions la terre

J'avais dans la nuit compté trois lumières
Le temps de dormir tout se confondait
Fils espoir et fleur miroir œil et lune
Homme sans saveur mais clair de langage
Femme sans éclat mais fluide aux doigts

Daddy of Ruins
Your son is dead
Assassinated

Daddy Hatred
O cruel victim
My comrade of two wars
Our life is ragged
Bleeding and ugly
But we swear soon
To take up arms

Daddy Hope
Hope of others
You are everywhere.

⊙

And the mother speaks :

I had built within our pledges three great castles
One for life one for death and one for love
    And like a treasure I hid
    The poor little sorrows
    Of my good and happy life

In gentleness I wove three mantles
One for us two and two for our child
    We had the same hands
    We thought one for the other
    And we made the earth beautiful

In the night I counted three lights
Sleep melted them together
Son hope and flower mirror eye and moon
Man without zest but clear of language
Woman without brilliance but fluid of the fingers

Brusquement c'est le désert
Et je me perds dans le noir
L'ennemi s'est révélé
Je suis seule pour aimer.
Je suis seule pour aimer.

⊙

Son fils, cet enfant...
Cet enfant aurait pu mentir
Et se sauver

La molle plaine infranchissable
Cet enfant n'aimait pas mentir
Il cria très fort ses forfaits
Il opposa sa vérité
La vérité
Comme une épée à ses bourreaux
Comme une épée sa loi suprême

Et ses bourreaux se sont vengés
Ils ont fait défiler la mort
L'espoir la mort l'espoir la mort
Ils l'ont grâcié puis ils l'ont tué

On l'avait durement traité
Ses pieds ses mains étaient brisés
Dit le gardien du cimetière.

⊙

Une seule pensée une seule passion
Et les armes de la douleur.

⊙

Des combattants saignant le feu
Ceux qui feront la paix sur terre
Des ouvriers des paysans
Des guerriers mêlés à la foule
Et quels prodiges de raison
Pour mieux frapper

92

Suddenly there is the wilderness
I lose myself in the darkness
The enemy is revealed
I am alone for loving.
I am alone for loving.

⊙

Her son, this child...
This child could have lied
And saved himself

The soft and insurmountable plain
This child did not care to lie
He cried aloud his crime
He opposed his truth
Truth
Like a sword to his butchers
Like a sword his supreme law

And his butchers took their revenge
Parading death before him
Hope death hope death
They pardoned him and then they killed him

They abused him terribly
His hands and feet were broken
Said the caretaker of the cemetery.

⊙

One single thought one single passion
And the weapons of sorrow.

⊙

Fighters bleeding fire
Those who will make peace on earth
Workers peasants
Warriors mingling with the masses
And what prodigies of reason
The better to strike

93

Des guerriers comme des ruisseaux
Partout sur les champs desséchés
Ou battant d'ailes acharnées
Le ciel boueux pour effacer
La morale de fin du monde
Des oppresseurs

Et selon l'amour la haine

Des guerriers selon l'espoir
Selon le sens de la vie
Et la commune parole
Selon la passion de vaincre
Et de réparer le mal
Qu'on nous a fait

Des guerriers selon mon cœur
Celui-ci pense à la mort
Celui-là n'y pense pas
L'un dort l'autre ne dort pas
Mais tous font le même rêve
Se libérer

Chacun est l'ombre de tous.

⊙

Les uns sombres les autres nus
Chantant leur bien mâchant leur mal
Mâchant le poids de leur corps
Ou chantant comme on s'envole

Par mille rêves humains
Par mille voies de nature
Ils sortent de leur pays
Et leur pays entre en eux
De l'air passe dans leur sang

94

Warriors like fresh streams
Running through dried-out fields
Or beating with implacable wings
The muddy sky to wipe away
The world's-end morality
Of the oppressors.

And according to the love the hatred

Warriors according to hope
According to the direction of life
And the mutual word
To the passion for conquering
And reparation of the evil
Which has been done us

Warriors according to my heart
This one thinks of death
The other does not think of it
One sleeps the other lies awake
But all have the same dream
To free themselves

Each one is the shadow of all.

⊙

Some somber others naked
Singing their good swallowing their misfortune
Swallowing the weight of their bodies
Or singing as one might fly

By a thousand human dreams
By a thousand ways of nature
They spring from their country
And their country enters into them
Air passes through their blood

Leur pays peut devenir
Le vrai pays des merveilles
Le Pays de l'Innocence.

Des réfractaires selon l'homme
Sous le ciel de tous les hommes
Sur la terre unie et pleine

Au dedans de ce fruit mûr
Le soleil comme un cœur pur
Tout le soleil pour les hommes

Tous les hommes pour les hommes
La terre entière et le temps
Le bonheur dans un seul corps.

Je dis ce que je vois
Ce que je sais
Ce qui est vrai.

☉

TUER

Il tombe cette nuit
Une étrange paix sur Paris
Une paix d'yeux aveugles
De rêves sans couleur
Qui se cognent aux murs
Une paix de bras inutiles
De fronts vaincus
D'hommes absents
De femmes déjà passées
Pâles froides et sans larmes

[1943]

Their country can become
A true land of miracles
A Land of Innocence

Insubmissive according to man
Beneath the sky of all men
On an earth full and united

Within this ripened fruit
The sun like a pure heart
All sunlight for mankind

All men for mankind
The entire earth and time
Happiness in a single body.

I say what I see
What I know
Which is true.

⊙

KILL

Tonight there falls
A strange peace over Paris
A peace of blind eyes
Of dreams without color
That hurl themselves against the walls
A peace of useless arms
Of vanquished faces
Of absent men
Of women already faded
Pale cold and tearless

Il tombe cette nuit
Dans le silence
Une étrange lueur sur Paris
Sur le bon vieux cœur de Paris
La lueur sourde du crime
Prémédité sauvage et pur
Du crime contre les bourreaux
Contre la mort.

☉

BETES ET MECHANTS

Venant du dedans
Venant du dehors
C'est nos ennemis
Ils viennent d'en haut
Ils viennent d'en bas
De près et de loin
De droite et de gauche
Habillés de vert
Habillés de gris
La veste trop courte
Le manteau trop long
La croix de travers
Grands de leurs fusils
Courts de leurs couteaux
Fiers de leurs espions
Forts de leurs bourreaux
Et gros de chagrin
Armés jusqu'à terre
Armés jusqu'en terre
Raides de saluts
Et raides de peur
Devant leurs bergers

[1943]

Tonight there falls
In the silence
A strange glow over Paris
Over the good old heart of Paris
The muffled glow of crime
Savage premeditated and pure
Crime against butchers
Against death.

⊙

STUPID AND EVIL

Coming from within
Coming from without
These our enemies
Coming from above
Coming from below
From near and far
From right and left
Dressed in green
Dressed in grey
The blouse too short
The overcoat too long
The cross askew
Their rifles long
Their knives short
Proud of their spies
Strong in their butchers
And heavy with dismay
Armed to the earth
Armed in the earth
Stiff with salutes
And stiff with fear
Before their shepherds

Imbibés de bière
Imbibés de lune
Chantant gravement
La chanson des bottes
Ils ont oublié
La joie d'être aimé
Quand ils disent oui
Tout leur répond non
Quand ils parlent d'or
Tout se fait de plomb
Mais contre leur ombre
Tout se fera d'or
Tout rajeunira
Qu'ils partent qu'ils meurent
Leur mort nous suffit.

Nous aimons les hommes
Ils s'évaderont
Nous en prendrons soin
Au matin de gloire
D'un monde nouveau
D'un monde à l'endroit.

⊙

D'UN SEUL POEME ENTRE LA VIE ET LA MORT

As-tu bien vu ton semblable
Comme il profite de tout
Il a la tête brillante
Il a la tête enflammée
Sous un masque de soleil
Sous un doux masque d'or double
Ses yeux sont des roses chaudes
Car ton semblable a bon cœur

Beer-soaked
Moon-soaked
Gravely singing
The song of boots
They have forgotten
The joy of being loved
When they say yes
All answer no
When they speak of gold
All turns to lead
But against their shadow
All will turn to gold
All will grow young again
Let them leave let them die
Their death suffices us

We love men
They shall escape
We shall take care of them
On the morning of glory
Of a new world
Of a world set right.

⊙

ONE POEM BETWEEN LIFE AND DEATH

Have you seen your fellow man
How he profits of everything
He has a brilliant head
A head in flames
Beneath a mask of sunlight
Beneath a soft mask of double gold
His eyes are hot roses
For your fellow man has a good heart

Il t'a montré le chemin
Vers la grille et vers la clé
Vers la porte à dépasser
Vers ta femme et tes enfants
Vers la place des visages
Il te rend la liberté

Mais je rêve et j'en ai honte
L'on va t'imposer la mort
La mort légère et puante
Qui ne répond qu'à la mort
Tout va d'un lieu grondant de vie vers le désert
La source de ton sang s'atténue disparaît
Nos ennemis ont besoin de tuer
Ils ont besoin d'être nos ennemis

Il n'y a rien d'essentiel à détruire
Qu'un homme après un homme
Il n'y a rien d'essentiel à créer
Que la vie tout entière en un seul corps
Que le respect de la vie et des morts
Qui sont morts pour la vie
Comme toi mon semblable
Qui n'as rien fait que de haïr la mort.

⊙

PENSEZ

Pensez aux lieux sans pudeur
Où des hommes sont reclus
Où les absents sont présents
Où les yeux sont sans reflets

102

[1944]

He has shown you the way
To the iron gate and to the key
To the door to pass beyond
To your wife and children
To the place of countenances
He gives you liberty

But I dream and I am ashamed of it
They are imposing death on you
Death light and putrid
Which answers only to death
All goes from a place rumbling with life toward
    the wilderness
The source of your blood dries up and disappears
Our enemies have need of killing
They have need of being our enemies

There is nothing essential to destroy
But one man after another
There is nothing essential to create
But a complete life in a single body
But the respect for life and for the dead
Who died for life
As you my fellow man
Who have done nothing but hate death.

⊙

THINK

Think of the places without modesty
Where the men are closed in
Where the absent are present
Where eyes are without reflection

Tout prend vite la couleur
Des muguets plats du plafond
Des blés bleus des surveillants
Muguets blés bleus en surface
En tristesse indélébile
Un peu de pain de l'eau sale

Pourquoi vivons-nous pourquoi
Annulons notre passé
Blasphémons notre avenir
Consolons-nous bêtement
Chantant Ceux qui sont à l'air
Ont trop l'air de pauvres hères

La liberté pourquoi faire
Pour nos maîtres pas pour nous
Pour nous tenir dans les fers
Pour nous tenir dans le vide
Pour nous vaincre et nous apprendre
A consentir sans la grande
Raison qui fait l'homme grand

Sans la Raison fraternelle.

⊙

ON TE MENACE

On te menace de la guerre
On te menace de la paix
On expose ton cœur aux coups
Quant à ton corps on ose à peine
En parler tant on lui en veut
Quels sales ennemis tu as

[1944]

Everything quickly takes the color
Of the drab lilies of the ceiling
Of the blue wheat of watchers
Lilies and wheat blue on the surface
In indelible sorrow
A little bread a little dirty water

Why do we live why
Let us annul our past
Blaspheme our future
Console ourselves stupidly
Singing Those who are outside
Have too much a pauper look

Liberty what for
For our mastérs not ourselves
For keeping us in irons
For keeping us in emptiness
For conquering us and teaching us
To give in without the great
Reason that makes man great

Without fraternal Reason.

☉

THEY THREATEN YOU

They threaten you with war
They threaten you with peace
They expose your heart to blows
And as for your body you hardly dare
Speak of it so much it is begrudged
What rotten enemies you have

Pourtant tu aimes tes amis
Ta femme et le chant du matin
Pourtant ton visage s'éclaire
Quand tu le vois parmi les autres
Pourtant tu prends le bon vin
Pour du bon pain
Pourtant tu ne crois connaître
De créatures que parfaites
De créatures qu'aérées
De conquérantes que conquises
Amis amours sont réunis
Nos désirs gagneront sur nous

Des étoiles s'agglutinent
Sur tes paupières fermées
Dormeur vois la vie est vaine
Si de tout ne sort la vie

Tu rêves qu'un solitaire
Le dernier des solitaires
Le dernier de nos bons maîtres
S'éteint il manquait de tout

Et c'est le dernier coupable
Et c'est enfin notre fête.

⊙

A CELLE DONT ILS REVENT

Neuf cent mille prisonniers
Cinq cent mille politiques
Un million de travailleurs

Still you love your friends
Your wife and the song of morning
And still your face lights up
When you see it among the others
Still you drink good wine
With good bread
You still believe you know
Only perfect creatures
Aethereal creatures
Only conquered conquerors
Friends loves are reunited
Our desires will gain on us

Stars collect upon
Your closed eyelids
Sleeper see that life is vain
Unless life grows from everything

You dream that a solitary man
The last of the solitary men
The last of our good masters
Burns out he had nothing

And it is the final guilty one
And at last it is our holiday.

⊙

TO HER OF WHOM THEY DREAM

Nine hundred thousand prisoners of war
Five hundred thousand political prisoners
One million forced workers

Maîtresse de leur sommeil
Donne-leur des forces d'homme
Le bonheur d'être sur terre
Donne-leur dans l'ombre immense
Les lèvres d'un amour doux
Comme l'oubli des souffrances

Maîtresse de leur sommeil
Fille femme sœur et mère
Aux seins gonflés de baisers
Donne-leur notre pays
Tel qu'ils l'ont toujours chéri
Un pays fou de la vie

Un pays où le vin chante
Où les moissons ont bon cœur
Où les enfants sont malins
Où les vieillards sont plus fins
Qu'arbres à fruits blancs de fleurs
Où l'on peut parler aux femmes

Neuf cent mille prisonniers
Cinq cent mille politiques
Un million de travailleurs

Maîtresse de leur sommeil
Neige noire des nuits blanches
A travers un feu exsangue
Sainte Aube à la canne blanche
Fais-leur voir un chemin neuf
Hors de leur prison de planches

Ils sont payes pour connaître
Les pires forces du mal
Pourtant ils ont tenu bon
Ils sont criblés de vertus
Tout autant que de blessures
Car il faut qu'ils se survivent

[1944]

Mistress of their slumber
Give them the strength of men
The happiness of being on earth
In the immense shadow give them
The lips of a sweet love
Like the oblivion of suffering

Mistress of their slumber
Daughter wife sister and mother
With breasts swollen with kisses
Give them our country
Such as they have always loved it
A country mad with life

A country where the wine sings
Where the harvests have a good heart
Where the children are clever
Where the old men are finer
Than fruit trees white with blossoms
Where one may speak to women

Nine hundred thousand prisoners of war
Five hundred thousand political prisoners
One million forced workers

Mistress of their slumber
Black snow of white sleepless nights
Across a bloodless fire
Sainte Aube with the blindman's cane
Show them a new road
Out of their wooden prisons

They are paid to know
The worst forces of evil
Still they have held good
They are riddled with virtues
As many as they have wounds
For they must survive

[1944]

Maîtresse de leur repos
Maîtresse de leur éveil
Donne-leur la liberté
Mais garde-nous notre honte
D'avoir pu croire à la honte
Même pour l'anéantir.

⊙

LE POEME HOSTILE

Dans la souveraine inégalité
Au tour du maître de s'enfuir
Dévoré par la haine
Au tour du maître de monter
Sur sa galère d'or son vaisseau de fortune

Dévoré par la haine
Ce fruit d'où naît la roue la roue d'où naît la route
La route où naît un mort et la mort prend tournure
Dans le sang et la boue ce mort sans sépulture
Craquerait sous la dent d'un hiver plus sévère
Que voulait-il ce mort un peu manger et boire
Aimer rêver et rire sous un ciel clément
Dans la souveraine inégalité
Et dans l'herbe fraîche et fleurie d'aurore
Etre ce couple qui s'aimait sans y penser
Etre ce couple lourd de ventre et de plaisir
Dévoré par l'amour et qui chante très haut
Nous sommes la lumière et notre cœur rayonne
Nous sommes sur la terre et nous en profitons

[1944]

Mistress of their repose
Mistress of their awakenings
Give them liberty
But keep with us our shame
For having been able to believe in shame
Even to stifle it.

⊙

HOSTILE POEM

In sovereign inequality
The master in his turn takes flight
Devoured by hatred
It is the master's turn to board
His golden galley his makeshift vessel

Devoured by hatred
This fruit from which is born the wheel the wheel
    from which is born the road
The road where a corpse is born and death takes
    shape
In blood in filth this graveless corpse
Would crack beneath a colder winter's bite
What did this corpse want a little food and drink
To love and dream and laugh under a merciful sky
In sovereign inequality
And in grass fresh and flowered with dawn
To be this couple who loved without thinking of it
To be this couple heavy of womb and pleasure
Devoured by love and singing aloud
We are the light and our heart radiates
We are on earth and we profit of it

111

Tandis que celui-là dévoré par la haine
Est en proie à la terre aux hommes et aux bêtes
Et la terre et les hommes et les bêtes c'est lui
Entièrement dévoré par la haine

Le sang corrompu de la mort emplit son cœur
Le vertueux refus d'aimer glace son front.

⊙

COMPRENNE QUI VOUDRA

En ce temps-là, pour ne pas châtier les coupables,
on maltraitait des filles. On allait même jusqu'à
les tondre.

Comprenne qui voudra
Moi mon remords ce fut
La malheureuse qui resta
Sur le pavé
La victime raisonnable
A la robe déchirée
Au regard d'enfant perdue
Découronnée défigurée
Celle qui ressemble aux morts
Qui sont morts pour être aimés

Une fille faite pour un bouquet
Et couverte
Du noir crachat des ténèbres

Une fille galante
Comme une aurore de premier mai
La plus aimable bête

[1944]

While this man devoured by hatred
Is prey to earth to man and beast
And the earth and the men and the beasts are
    himself
Entirely devoured by hatred

The corrupt blood of death fills his heart
The virtuous refusal to love freezes his forehead.

☉

UNDERSTAND WHO WILL

*At that time, in order not to punish the guilty, they
maltreated the prostitutes. They even went so far
as to shave their heads.*

Understand who will
For me my remorse was
The poor girl left lying
On the pavement
The reasonable victim
With a torn dress
With the look of a lost child
Uncrowned disfigured
Who resembles the dead
Who died for being loved

A girl made for a bouquet
And covered
With the black spittle of shadows

A gallant girl
Like the dawn on a first of May
The most likeable animal

113

Souillée et qui n'a pas compris
Qu'elle est souillée
Une bête prise au piège
Des amateurs de beauté

Et ma mère la femme
Voudrait bien dorloter
Cette image idéale
De son malheur sur terre.

⊙

GABRIEL PERI

Un homme est mort qui n'avait pour défense
Que ses bras ouverts à la vie
Un homme est mort qui n'avait d'autre route
Que celle où l'on hait les fusils
Un homme est mort qui continue la lutte
Contre la mort contre l'oubli

Car tout ce qu'il voulait
Nous le voulions aussi
Nous le voulons aujourd'hui
Que le bonheur soit la lumière
Au fond des yeux au fond du cœur
Et la justice sur la terre

Il y a des mots qui font vivre
Et ce sont des mots innocents
Le mot chaleur le mot confiance
Amour justice et le mot liberté
Le mot enfant et le mot gentillesse
Et certains noms de fleurs et certains noms de
    fruits

Soiled and who has not understood
That she is soiled
Animal caught in the trap
Of the lovers of beauty

And my mother the woman
Would have cradled in her arms
This ideal image
Of her misery on earth.

⊙

GABRIEL PERI *

A man is dead who had for his defense
Only his arms opened to life
A man is dead who had no road other
Than the one where rifles are hated
A man is dead who continues the struggle
Against death against oblivion

For all he wanted
We too wanted
We want today
That happiness be the light
In the depths of eyes the depths of hearts
And justice on the earth

There are words which give life
And they are innocent words
The word warmth the word confidence
Love justice and the word liberty
The word child and the word kindness
And certain names of flowers and certain names
    of fruits

[1944]

Le mot courage et le mot découvrir
Et le mot frère et le mot camarade
Et certains noms de pays de villages
Et certains noms de femmes et d'amis
Ajoutons-y Péri
Péri est mort pour ce qui nous fait vivre
Tutoyons-le sa poitrine est trouée
Mais grâce à lui nous nous connaissons mieux
Tutoyons-nous son espoir est vivant

The word courage and the word discover
The word brother and the word comrade
And certain names of countries and villages
And certain names of women and of friends
Let us add Péri to them
Péri is dead for that which makes us live
Speak to him as a brother his breast is riddled
But thanks to him we know each other better
Speak to each other as brothers his hope is living.

* Péri was an editor of l'*Humanité* and vice-president of the Foreign Commission of the Chamber of Deputies. He was shot by the Germans on December 15, 1941. Bribed and tortured, Péri did not renounce his principles, and in his last letter, he wrote : « Let my friends know that I have remained faithful to the ideal of my life, let my countrymen know that I am going to die so that France may live. For the last time, I have looked into my conscience. The result is positive. If I had to begin my life over again, I would follow the same road. Tonight, more than any other night, I believe that my dear friend Paul Vaillant-Couturier was right when he said that : « Communism is the youth of the world' and that it, prepares for singing tomorows ». In a little while I am going to prepare for · singing tomorows. I feel myself strong in the face of death. Goodby, and long live France. »

CHARNIERS

L'aube est sortie d'un coupe-gorge
L'aube noircit sur des décombres
Se fond parmi des ombres molles
Parmi d'abjectes nourritures
Parmi de repugnants secrets

Où sont les rires et les rêves
Où est le bouquet de la peau
Où est le mouvement constant
La roue du soleil et des sèves

Des racines aromatiques
Séparent les chairs corrompues
Le cœur n'est plus l'image insigne
L'aube n'arrose plus la boue
Elle est le poison du chaos

Où sont les flammes et la sueur
Où sont les larmes et le sang
Où sont le regard et la voix
Où est le cri de ralliement

Comprendre gît sous la vermine
Sous le bruit ruminant des mouches
Le ciel la terre se limitent
A la destruction de l'homme
Voir clair ne sonne que ténèbres

Ténèbres des passants se hâtent
Pour mieux retrouver leurs ténèbres
Intactes pleines à craquer
De ce vieux pus des bienheureux
Qui contredit toute famine
Qui nie le mal et les tortures

CHARNEL HOUSE

Dawn has risen from a den of infamy
Dawn darkens over the ruins
And melts among soft shadows
Among abject nourishment
Among repugnant secrets

Where are the laughter and the dreams
The sweet odor of the skin
Where is the constant motion
The wheel of the sun and the sap of trees

Aromatic roots
Separate the corrupted flesh
The heart no longer is the signal image
Dawn no longer waters the mire
It is the poison of chaos

Where are the flames and the sweat
Where are the tears and the blood
Where are the look and the voice
Where is the rallying cry

Understanding lies beneath the vermin
Beneath the ruminant sound of flies
Earth and sky limit themselves
To the destruction of men
Clear seeing rings only shadows

Shadows the passers-by hasten
The better to find their shadows
Intact filled to bursting
With this old pus of the blessed
Which contradicts all famine
Which denies the evil and the tortures

119

Ténèbres les bourreaux sont loin
Et leurs complices se délassent
Regards aveugles fronts éteints
Bijoux couvrant un trou puant
Fleurs de calcul étoiles basses
Oubli commode oubli sublime

Trésor amassé sans dégoût
Par les gagnants de la défaite
Petits profits grandes ruines
Ténèbres ignorées des vers
Précieuse cendre au fond des poches
L'avenir tient à quelques sous

Une vie large vaut sa honte
Le froid chante comme un voleur
Et les vieux crimes tiennent chaud
Les bourreaux justifiaient la mort
Ils économisaient le temps
Ils n'avaient pas peur des enfants

Mais sur la nuit fille de l'homme
La revanche d'amour rayonne
L'aube est tissée de fils limpides
Les innocents ont reparu
Légers d'air pur blancs de colère
Forts de leur droit impérissable

Forts d'une terre sans défauts.

Shadows the butchers are far
Their accomplices are at rest
Blind looks extinguished faces
Jewels covering a stinking hole
Flowers of calculation low stars
Convenient oblivion sublime oblivion

Treasure piled up without disgust
By the winners of defeat
Small profits great ruins
Shadows unknown to worms
Treasured ashes in the bottom of pockets
The future hangs on a few pennies

A full life is worth its shame
The cold sings like a thief
The old crimes keep you warm
The butchers justified death
They saved time
They were not afraid of children

But in the night daughter of man
Shines love's revenge
The dawn is woven with clear threads
The innocent have reappeared
Light with pure air white with rage
Strong in their imperishable right

Strong in a faultless earth.

LE MEME JOUR POUR TOUS

I

L'épée qu'on n'enfonce pas dans le cœur des maî-
    tres des coupables
On l'enfonce dans le cœur des pauvres et des
    innocents

Les premiers yeux sont d'innocence
Et les seconds de pauvreté
Il faut savoir les protéger

Je ne veux condamner l'amour
Que si je ne tue pas la haine
Et ceux qui me l'ont inspirée

II

Un petit oiseau marche dans d'immenses régions
Où le soleil a des ailes

III

Elle riait autour de moi
Autour de moi elle était nue

Elle était comme une forêt
Comme une foule de femmes
Autour de moi
Comme une armure contre le désert
Comme une armure contre l'injustice

122

THE SAME DAY FOR ALL

I

The sword we do not sink in the heart of the guilty's
    masters
We sink in the heart of the poor and innocent

The first eyes are of innocence
The second of poverty
We must know how to protect them

I will condemn love only
If I do not kill hate
And those who have inspired me with it

II

A small bird walks in the vast regions
Where the sun has wings

III

Her laughter was about me
About me she was naked

She was like a forest
Like a multitude of women
About me
Like an armor against wilderness
Like an armor against injustice

L'injustice frappait partout
Etoile unique étoile inerte d'un ciel gras qui est la
     privation de la lumière
L'injustice frappait les innocents et les héros les
     insensés
Qui sauront un jour régner

Car je les entendais rire
Dans leur sang dans leur beauté
Dans la misère et les tortures
Rire d'un rire à venir
Rire à la vie et naître au rire.

19 *Novembre*, 1944.

☉

CHANT DU FEU VAINQUEUR DU FEU

Ce feu prenait dans la chair
Et l'aube était son égale
Ce feu prenait dans les mains
Dans le regard dans la voix
Il me faisait avancer
Et je brûlais le désert
Et je caressais ce feu
Feu de terre et de terreur
Contre les terreurs de la nuit
Contre les terreurs de la cendre
Un feu comme une ligne droite
Un feu fatal dans les ténèbres
Comme un pas dans la poussière
Un feu vocal et capital
Qui criait par dessus les toits

Au feu la mort

Injustice struck everywhere
Unique star inert star of a thick sky which is the
    privation of light
Injustice struck the innocent the heroes and the
    madmen
Who shall one day know how to rule

For I heard them laugh
In their blood in their beauty
In misery and torture
Laugh of a laugh to come
Laughter at life and birth in laughter.

November 19, 1944.

⊙

SONG OF FIRE CONQUEROR OF FIRE

This fire caught in the flesh
And the dawn was its equal
This fire caught in the hands
In the look in the voice
It made me go forward
And I burned the wilderness
And I caressed this fire
Fire of earth and terror
Against the terrors of night
Against the terrors of ashes
Fire like a straight line
Fatal fire in the shadows
Like a footstep in the dust
Vocal and capital fire
Which cried from the rooftops

To the fire with death

Ce feu prenait dans la chair
Ce feu s'en prenaît aux chaînes
Aux chaînes et aux murs aux bâillons aux serrures
Aux aveugles aux larmes
Aux naissances infirmes
A la mort que j'avais méchamment mise au
    monde
Un feu qui s'attaquait aux étoiles éteintes
Aux ailes chues aux fleurs fanées
Un feu qui s'attaquait aux ruines
Un feu qui réparait les désastres du feu
Sans ombres sans victimes
Buisson de sang et d'air
Moisson de cris sublimes
Et moisson de rayons
Dans la fronde d'un hymne

Un feu sans créateur

Derrière lui la rosée
Derrière lui le printemps
Derrière lui les enfants
Qui font croire à tous les hommes
A leur cœur indivisible
A leur cœur immaculé
Un feu clair jusqu'à l'essence
De toutes les formes nues
Un feu clair dans le filet
Des lueurs et des couleurs
Feu de vue et de parole
Caresse perpétuelle
Amour espoir de nature
Connaissance par l'espoir
Rêve où rien n'est inventé

Rêve entier vertu du feu.

This fire caught in the flesh
This fire laid blame on the chains
On chains on walls on gags on locks
On blindmen on tears
On crippled births
On death which I had wickedly brought into the
    world
A fire which attacked the burnt-out stars
The fallen wings the faded flowers
A fire which attacked ruins
A fire which repaired the disasters of fire
Without shadows without victims
Bush of blood and air
Harvest of sublime cries
Harvest of sunlight
In the sling of an anthem

A fire without creator

Behind it the dew
Behind it the springtime
Behind it the children
Who make all men believe
In their indivisible heart
In their immaculate heart
A clear fire in the essence
Of all naked shapes
Clear fire in the net
Of lights and colors
Fire of sight and speech
Perpetual caress
Love hope of nature
Knowledge by hope
Dream where nothing is invented

Entire dream virtue of fire.

A L'ECHELLE HUMAINE

A la mémoire du colonel Fabien et à Laurent Casa-
nova qui m'a si bien parlé de lui.

On a tué un homme
Un homme un ancien enfant
Dans un grand paysage
Une tache de sang
Comme un soleil couchant
Un homme couronné
De femmes et d'enfants
Tout un idéal d'homme
Pour notre éternité

Il est tombé
Et son cœur s'est vidé
Ses yeux se sont vidés
Sa tête s'est vidée
Ses mains se sont ouvertes
Sans une plainte
Car il croyait au bonheur
Des autres
Car il avait répété
Je t'aime sur tous les tons
A sa mère à sa gardienne
A sa complice à son alliée
A la vie
Et il allait au combat
Contre les bourreaux des siens
Contre l'idée d'ennemi

Et même les pires jours
Il avait chéri sa peine
Sa nature était d'aimer
Et de respecter la vie
Sa nature était la mienne

[1945]

THE HUMAN MEASURE

To the memory of Colonel Fabien * *and to Laurent
Casanova who spoke so well of him to me.*

They have killed a man
A man a sometime child
On a wide countryside
A bloodstain
Like a setting sun
A man crowned
With women and children
A completely ideal man
For our eternity

He is fallen
And his heart is emptied
His eyes are emptied
His head is emptied
His hands have opened
Without complaint
For he believed in the happiness
Of others
For he had repeated
I love you in every tone
To his mother to his governess
To his helpmate to his ally
To life
And he did battle
Against the butchers of his people
Against the idea of enemy

Even in the worst days
He cherished his sorrow
His nature was to love
To respect life
His nature was my own

Rien qu'un seul jet de courage
Rien que la grandeur du peuple
Et je t'aime finit mal
Mais il affirme la vie
Je t'aime c'était l'Espagne
Qui luttait pour le soleil
C'est la région parisienne
Avec ses chemins puérils
Avec ses enfants gentils
Et le premier attentat
Contre les soldats du mal
Contre la mort répugnante
C'est la première lumière
Dans la nuit des malheureux
Lumière toujours première
Toujours parfaite

Lumière de relation
Ronde de plus en plus souple
Etendue et animée
Graine et fleur et fruit et graine
Et je t'aime finit bien
Pour les hommes de demain.

Nothing more than a single flash of courage
Nothing more than the greatness of a people
And I love you turns out badly
But it affirms life
I love you it was Spain
Struggling for sunlight
It is all of Paris
With her childlike pathways
With her gentle children
And the first attack
Against the soldiers of evil
Against repugnant death
It is the first light
In the night of the unhappy
Light always first
Always perfect

Light of respect
Round more and more supple
Drawn out and animated
Seed and flower fruit and seed
And I love you turns out well
For the men of tomorrow.

---

* Of Colonel Fabien, Paul Eluard writes : « At the age of seventeen, Fabien enlisted in the International Brigade and fought in Spain until he was severely wounded in the abdomen. After his return to France, he became Secretary of the *Jeunesses Communistes de la Région Parisienne.* From the first months of the Occupation, Fabien again took up his combat post. Far and wide, he gave the signal of revolt. By the end of 1941, he had organized 80% of the actions of the Resistance. While chief of staff of a combat group, his head was pierced by a bullet. Scarcely convalescent, he was taken prisoner and horribly tortured. He escaped. During the Paris insurrection, commanding eight tanks, he liquidated the strong-point at the Jardins de Luxembourg. Later, he went to the Ardennes where he had the responsibility of defending a twelve-kilometer front. It was there that he was killed. In 1942, Fabien's father was shot to death and his wife deported to Auschwitz. He is survived by five children. » Tr.

LES VENDEURS D'INDULGENCE

Ceux qui ont oublié le mal au nom du bien
Ceux qui n'ont pas de cœur nous prêchent le
    pardon
Les criminels leur sont indispensables
Ils croient qu'il faut de tout pour faire un monde.

    Ecoutez-les ils prêchent haut
    Nul n'ose plus les faire taire
    Ils ont des droits écoutez-les
    Ecoutez cet écho d'hier

    Qu'il résiste ou qu'il capitule
    Un général en vaut un autre
    Des Français habillés en vert
    Sont quand même de fiers soldats
    De bons canons pour l'ennemi
    Sont quand même de bons canons
    Et plus il possède d'esclaves
    Plus le maître a de raisons d'être.

Les femmes d'Auschwitz les petits enfants Juifs
Les terroristes à l'œil juste les otages
Ne pouvaient pas savoir par quel hideux miracle
La clémence serait ardemment invoquée.

Il n'y a pas de pierre plus précieuse
Que le désir de venger l'innocent

Il n'y a pas de ciel plus éclatant
Que le matin où les traîtres succombent

Il n'y a pas de salut sur terre
Tant que l'on peut pardonner aux bourreaux.

132

[1945]

THE SELLERS OF INDULGENCES

Those who have forgotten evil in the name of good
Those who have no heart preach pardon to us
Criminals are indispensable to them
They believe it takes all kinds to make a world.

Listen to them they preach aloud
And none dares silence them
They have their rights listen to them
Listen to this echo of yesterday

Whether he resists whether he surrenders
One general is worth another
And Frenchmen dressed in green
Are still proud soldiers
Good cannon for the enemy
Are still good cannon
And the more slaves the master has
The more reasons to be master

The women of Auschwitz the little Jewish children
Terrorists with a sharp eye the hostages
Could not know by what hideous miracle
Mercy would be ardently invoked.

There is no stone more precious
Than the desire to avenge the innocent

There is no sky more brilliant
Than the morning of a traitor's death

And there is no health on earth
While butchers can be pardoned.

FAIRE VIVRE

Ils étaient quelques-uns qui vivaient dans la nuit
En rêvant du ciel caressant
Ils étaient quelques-uns qui aimaient la forêt
Et qui croyaient au bois brûlant
L'odeur des fleurs les ravissait même de loin
La nudité de leurs désirs les recouvrait

Ils joignaient dans leur cœur le souffle mesuré
A ce rien d'ambition de la vie naturelle
Qui grandit dans l'été comme un été plus fort

Ils joignaient dans leur cœur l'espoir du temps qui
        vient
Et qui salue même de loin un autre temps
A des amours plus obstinées que le désert

Un tout petit peu de sommeil
Les rendait au soleil futur
Ils duraient ils savaient que vivre perpétue

Et leurs besoins obscurs engendraient la clarté.

⊙

Ils n'étaient que quelques-uns
Ils furent foule soudain

Ceci est de tous les temps.

TO MAKE LIVE

There were some who lived in the night
Dreaming of a caressing sky
There were some who loved the forest
Who believed in the burning wood
The smell of flowers delighted them even from afar
The nakedness of their desires covered them

In their hearts they joined the measured breath
To this nothing of ambition of a natural life
Which grows in summer as a stronger summer

In their hearts they joined the hope of time to come
Which even from afar salutes another time
To loves more headstrong than the wilderness

A little bit of sleep
Brought back their future sun
They lasted and they knew that living does
    continue

And their shadowy needs begot the light.

⊙

They were only a few
Suddenly they were a multitude

This is of all times.

LIBERTE

Sur mes cahiers d'écolier
Sur mon pupitre et les arbres
Sur le sable sur la neige
J'écris ton nom

Sur toutes les pages lues
Sur toutes les pages blanches
Pierre sang papier ou cendre
J'écris ton nom

Sur les images dorées
Sur les armes des guerriers
Sur la couronne des rois
J'écris ton nom

Sur la jungle et le désert
Sur les nids sur les genêts
Sur l'écho de mon enfance
J'écris ton nom

Sur les merveilles des nuits
Sur le pain blanc des journées
Sur les saisons fiancées
J'écris ton nom

Sur tous mes chiffons d'azur
Sur l'étang soleil moisi
Sur le lac lune vivante
J'écris ton nom

Sur les champs sur l'horizon
Sur les ailes des oiseaux
Et sur le moulin des ombres
J'écris ton nom

136

LIBERTY

On my schoolboy's notebooks
On my desk and on the trees
On sand on snow
I write your name

On all pages read
On all blank pages
Stone blood paper or ash
I write your name

On gilded images
On the weapons of warriors
On the crowns of kings
I write your name

On jungle and desert
On nests on gorse
On the echo of my chilhood
I write your name

On the wonders of nights
On the white bread of days
On betrothed seasons
I write your name

On all my rags of azure
On the pool musty sun
On the lake living moon
I write your name

On fields on the horizon
On the wings of birds
And on the mill of shadows
I write your name

Sur chaque bouffée d'aurore
Sur la mer sur les bateaux
Sur la montagne démente
J'écris ton nom

Sur la mousse des nuages
Sur les sueurs de l'orage
Sur la pluie épaisse et fade
J'écris ton nom

Sur les formes scintillantes
Sur les cloches des couleurs
Sur la vérité physique
J'écris ton nom

Sur les sentiers éveillés
Sur les routes déployées
Sur les places qui débordent
J'écris ton nom

Sur la lampe qui s'allume
Sur la lampe qui s'éteint
Sur mes maisons réunies
J'écris ton nom

Sur le fruit coupé en deux
Du miroir et de ma chambre
Sur mon lit coquille vide
J'écris ton nom

Sur mon chien gourmand et tendre
Sur ses oreilles dressées
Sur sa patte maladroite
J'écris ton nom

Sur le tremplin de ma porte
Sur les objets familiers

On each puff of dawn
On the sea on ships
On the demented mountain
I write your name

On the foam of clouds
On the sweat of storm
On thick insipid rain
I write your name

On shimmering shapes
On bells of color
On physical truth
I write your name

On awakened pathways
On roads spread out
On overflowing squares
I write your name

On the lamp that is lit
On the lamp that burns out
On my reunited houses
I write your name

On the fruit cut in two
Of the mirror and my chamber
On my bed empty shell
I write your name

On my dog greedy and tender
On his trained ears
On his awkward paw
I write your name

On the springboard of my door
On familiar objects

Sur le flot du feu béni
J'écris ton nom

Sur toute chair accordée
Sur le front de mes amis
Sur chaque main qui se tend
J'écris ton nom

Sur la vitre des surprises
Sur les lèvres attentives
Bien au-dessus du silence
J'écris ton nom

Sur mes refuges détruits
Sur mes phares écroulés
Sur les murs de mon ennui
J'écris ton nom

Sur l'absence sans désir
Sur la solitude nue
Sur les marches de la mort
J'écris ton nom

Sur la santé revenue
Sur le risque disparu
Sur l'espoir sans souvenir
J'écris ton nom

Et par le pouvoir d'un mot
Je recommence ma vie
Je suis né pour te connaître
Pour te nommer

Liberté.

On the flood of blessed fire
I write your name

On all tuned flesh
On the foreheads of my friends
On each hand outstretched
I write your name

On the window of surprises
On the attentive lips
Well above silence
I write your name

On my destroyed refuges
On my crumbled beacons
On the walls of my weariness
I write your name

On absence without desire
On naked solitude
On the steps of death
I write your name

On health returned
On the risk disappeared
On hope without memory
I write your name

And by the power of a word
I start my life again
I was born to know you
To name you

Liberty.

UN FEU SANS TACHE

La menace sous le ciel rouge
Venait d'en bas des mâchoires
Des écailles des anneaux
D'une chaîne glissante et lourde

La vie était distribuée
Largement pour que la mort
Prît au sérieux le tribut
Qu'on lui payait sans compter

La mort était le dieu d'amour
Et les vainqueurs dans un baiser
S'évanouissaient sur leurs victimes
La pourriture avait du cœur

Et pourtant sous le ciel rouge
Sous les appétits de sang
Sous la famine lugubre
La caverne se ferma

La terre utile effaça
Les tombes creusées d'avance
Les enfants n'eurent plus peur
Des profondeurs maternelles

Et la bêtise et la démence
Et la bassesse firent place
A des hommes frères des hommes
Ne luttant plus contre la vie

A des hommes indestructibles.

A FIRE WITHOUT STAIN

The threat beneath the red sky
Came from below the jaws
The scales the links
Of a chain slippery and heavy

Life was distributed
Widely so that death
Might take seriously the tribute
We paid it without reckoning

Death was the god of love
And the victors in a kiss
Fainted on their victims
And rot took heart

And still beneath the red sky
Beneath the appetites for blood
Beneath a baleful famine
The cavern closed

The useful earth erased
The tombs dug in advance
Children no longer were afraid
Of the maternal depths

And stupidity and madness
And baseness gave way
To men brothers of men
No longer struggling against life

To indestructible men.

BIENTOT

De tous les printemps du monde
Celui-ci est le plus laid
Entre toutes mes façons d'être
La confiante est la meilleure

L'herbe soulève la neige
Comme la pierre d'un tombeau
Moi je dors dans la tempête
Et je m'éveille les yeux clairs

Le lent le petit temps s'achève
Où toute rue devait passer
Par mes plus intimes retraites
Pour que je rencontre quelqu'un

Je n'entends pas parler les monstres
Je les connais ils ont tout dit
Je ne vois que les beaux visages
Les bons visages sûrs d'eux-mêmes

Sûrs de ruiner bientôt leurs maîtres.

⊙

LA HALTE DES HEURES

Immenses mots dits doucement
Grand soleil les volets fermés
Un grand navire au fil de l'eau
Ses voiles partageant le vent

144

SOON

Of all the springtimes of the world
This is the ugliest
Among all my ways of being
The confident is the best

The grass lifts up the snow
Like the stone of a tomb
But I sleep in the tempest
And I awaken with clear eyes

The slow the short time ends
Where all streets had to pass
By my most intimate retreats
So that I may meet someone

I do not hear the monsters speak
I know them they have said all
I see only the fine faces
The good faces sure of themselves

Sure soon to ruin their masters.

⊙

THE HALT OF HOURS

Immense words spoken softly
Strong sunlight the shutters closed
A great ship on the thread of water
Its sails sharing the wind

145

Bouche bien faite pour cacher
Une autre bouche et le serment
De ne rien dire qu'à deux voix
Du secret qui raye la nuit

Le seul rêve des innocents
Un seul murmure un seul matin
Et les saisons à l'unisson
Colorant de neige et de feu

Une foule enfin réunie.

⊙

COUVRE-FEU

Que voulez-vous la porte était gardée
Que voulez-vous nous étions enfermés
Que voulez-vous la rue était barrée
Que voulez-vous la ville était matée
Que voulez-vous elle était affamée
Que voulez-vous nous étions désarmés
Que voulez-vous la nuit était tombée
Que voulez-vous nous nous sommes aimés.

⊙

DRESSE PAR LA FAMINE

Dressé par la famine
L'enfant répond toujours je mange
Viens-tu je mange
Dors-tu je mange.

146

Mouth well made to hide
Another mouth and the pledge
To speak only with two voices
Of the secret which streaks the night

The single dream of the innocent
A single murmur a single morning
And the seasons together
Coloring with snow and fire

A multitude at last united.

☉

CURFEW

What did you expect the door was guarded
What did you expect we were locked in
What did you expect the street was barred
What did you expect the city was in check
What did you expect it was starving
What did you expect we were disarmed
What did you expect the night had fallen
What did you expect we were in love.

☉

TRAINED BY FAMINE

Trained by famine
The child always answers I am eating
Are you coming I am eating
Are you sleeping I am eating.

DU DEHORS

La nuit le froid la solitude
On m'enferma soigneusement
Mais les branches cherchaient leur voie dans la
    prison
Autour de moi l'herbe trouva le ciel
On verrouilla le ciel
Ma prison s'écroula
Le froid vivant le froid brûlant m'eut bien en main.

⊙

LA DERNIERE NUIT

I

Ce petit monde meurtrier
Est orienté vers l'innocent
Lui ôte le pain de la bouche
Et donne sa maison au feu
Lui prend sa veste et ses souliers
Lui prend son temps et ses enfants

Ce petit monde meurtrier
Confond les morts et les vivants
Blanchit la boue gracie les traîtres
Transforme la parole en bruit.

Merci minuit douze fusils
Rendent la paix à l'innocent
Et c'est aux foules d'enterrer
Sa chair sanglante et son ciel noir
Et c'est aux foules de comprendre
La faiblesse des meurtriers.

148

[1942]

FROM THE OUTSIDE

The night the cold the solitude
Carefully they locked me in
But the branches sought their way in the prison
About me grass found sky
They bolted out the sky
My prison crumbled
The living cold the burning cold had me well in
    hand.

⊙

THE LAST NIGHT

I

This murderous little world
Is oriented toward the innocent
Takes the bread from his mouth
Gives his house to the flames
Takes his coat and his shoes
Takes his time and his children

This murderous little world
Confounds the dead and living
Whitens the mud pardons traitors
And turns the word to noise

Thanks midnight twelve rifles
Restore peace to the innocent
And it is for the multitudes to bury
His bleeding flesh his black sky
And it is for the multitudes to understand
The frailty of murderers.

II

Le prodige serait une légère poussée contre le mur
Ce serait de pouvoir secouer cette poussière
Ce serait d'être unis.

III

Ils avaient mis à vif ses mains courbé son dos
Ils avaient creusé un trou dans sa tête
Et pour mourir il avait dû souffrir
Toute sa vie

IV

Beauté créée pour les heureux
Beauté tu cours un grand danger

Ces mains croisées sur tes genoux
Sont les outils d'un assassin

Cette bouche chantant très haut
Sert de sébile au mendiant

Et cette coupe de lait pur
Devient le sein d'une putain.

V

Les pauvres ramassaient leur pain dans le ruisseau
Leur regard couvrait la lumière
Et ils n'avaient plus peur la nuit

150

II

The wonder would be a light push against the wall
It would be being able to shake this dust
It would be to be united.

III

They had skinned his hands bent his back
They had dug a hole in his head
And to die he had to suffer
All his life.

IV

Beauty created for the happy
Beauty you run a great risk

These hands crossed on your knees
Are the tools of an assassin

This mouth singing aloud
Serves as a beggar's bowl

And this cup of pure milk
Becomes the breast of a whore.

V

The poor picked their bread from the gutter
Their look covered light
No longer were they afraid at night

151

Très faibles leur faiblesse les faisait sourire
Dans le fond de leur ombre ils emportaient leur
    corps
Ils ne se voyaient plus qu'à travers leur détresse
Ils ne se servaient plus que d'un langage intime
Et j'entendais parler doucement prudemment
D'un ancien espoir grand comme la main

J'entendais calculer
Les dimensions multipliées de la feuille d'automne
La fonte de la vague au sein de la mer calme
J'entendais calculer
Les dimensions multipliées de la force future.

VI

Je suis né derrière une façade affreuse
J'ai mangé j'ai ri j'ai rêvé j'ai eu honte
J'ai vécu comme un ombre
Et pourtant j'ai su chanter le soleil
Le soleil entier celui qui respire
Dans chaque poitrine et dans tous les yeux
La goutte de candeur qui luit après les larmes.

VII

Nous jetons le fagot des ténèbres au feu
Nous brisons les serrures rouillées de l'injustice
Des hommes vont venir qui n'ont plus peur d'eux-
    mêmes
Car ils sont sûrs de tous les hommes
Car l'ennemi à figure d'homme disparaît.

152

So weak their weakness made them smile
In the depths of their shadow they carried their
    body
They saw themselves only through their distress
They used only an intimate language
And I heard them speak gently prudently
Of an old hope big as a hand

I heard them calculate
The multiplied dimensions of the autumn leaf
The melting of the wave on the breast of a calm sea
I heard them calculate
The multiplied dimensions of the future force.

VI

I was born behind a hideous facade
I have eaten I have laughed I have dreamed I have
    been ashamed
I have lived like a shadow
Yet I knew how to sing the sun
The entire sun which breathes
In every breast and in all eyes
The drop of candor which sparkles after tears.

VII

We throw the faggot of shadows to the fire
We break the rusted locks of injustice
Men will come who will no longer fear themselves
For they are sure of all men
For the enemy with a man's face disappears.

LA VICTOIRE DE GUERNICA

1

Beau monde des masures
De la mine et des champs

2

Visages bons au feu visages bons au froid
Aux refus à la nuit aux injures aux coups

3

Visages bons à tout
Voici le vide qui vous fixe
Votre mort va servir d'exemple

4

La mort cœur renversé

5

Ils vous font payer le pain
Le ciel la terre l'eau le sommeil
Et la misère
De votre vie

6

Ils disaient désirer la bonne intelligence
Ils rationnaient les forts jugeaient les fous
Faisaient l'aumône partageaient un sou en deux
Ils saluaient les cadavres
Ils s'accablaient de politesses

7

Ils persévèrent ils exagèrent ils ne sont pas de notre
monde

154

[1938]

THE VICTORY OF GUERNICA

1

Fine world of ruins
Of mine of fields

2

Faces good in the fire faces good in the cold
In the denial of night of curses of blows

3

Faces good for everything
Here is the void which stares at you
Your death will serve example

4

Death a heart upturned

5

They make you pay for bread
For sky for earth water and sleep
And the misery
Of your life

6

They said desire the good intelligence
They rationed the strong judged the mad
Begged alms split a penny in two
They did homage to the corpses
They overwhelmed themselves with politeness

7

They persevere they exaggerate they are not of our
world

155

8

Les femmes les enfants ont le même trésor
De feuilles vertes de printemps et de lait pur
Et de durée
Dans leurs yeux purs

9

Les femmes les enfants ont le même trésor
Dans les yeux
Les hommes le défendent comme ils peuvent

10

Les femmes les enfants ont les mêmes roses rouges
Dans les yeux
Chacun montre son sang

11

La peur et le courage de vivre et de mourir
La mort si difficile et si facile

12

Hommes pour qui ce trésor fut chanté
Hommes pour qui ce trésor fut gâché

13

Hommes réels pour qui le désespoir
Alimente le feu dévorant de l'espoir
Ouvrons ensemble le dernier bourgeon de l'avenir

14

Parias la mort la terre et la hideur
De nos ennemis ont la couleur
Monotone de notre nuit
Nous en aurons raison.

8

The women the children have the same treasure
Of green leaves of spring and of pure milk
And of duration
In their pure eyes

9

The women the children have the same treasure
In their eyes
The men defend it as best they can

10

The women the children have the same red roses
In their eyes
Each one shows his blood

11

Fear and the courage to live and die
Death so difficult and so easy

12

Men for whom this treasure was sung
Men for whom this treasure was spoiled

13

Real men for whom despair
Feeds the devouring fire of hope
Let us open the final bud of the future together

14

Pariahs death earth and the horror
Of our enemies have
The monotonous color of our night
We will be right.

POESIE ININTERROMPUE

La résistance s'organise sur tous les fronts purs.

Tristan Tzara (*L'Antitête*, 1933).

*Je dédie ces pages à ceux qui les liront mal et à
ceux qui ne les aimeront pas.*

Paul Eluard.

. . . .

Nue effacée ensommeillée
Choisie sublime solitaire
Profonde oblique matinale
Fraîche nacrée ébouriffée
Ravivée première régnante
Coquette vive passionnée
Orangée rose bleuissante
Jolie mignonne délurée
Naturelle couchée debout
Etreinte ouverte rassemblée
Rayonnante désaccordée
Gueuse rieuse ensorceleuse
Etincelante ressemblante
Sourde secrète souterraine
Aveugle rude désastreuse
Boisée herbeuse ensanglantée
Sauvage obscure balbutiante
Ensoleillée illuminée
Fleurie confuse caressante
Instruite discrète ingénieuse
Fidèle facile étoilée
Charnue opaque palpitante
Inatérable contractée
Pavée construite vitrifiée
Globale haute populaire
Barrée gardée contradictoire

[1946]

UNINTERRUPTED POETRY

The resistance is organized on all pure foreheads.

Tristan Tzara (*L'Antitête*, 1933).

I dedicate these pages to those who will read them badly and to those who will not like them.

Paul Eluard.

. . . .

Naked obliterated slumbering
Selected sublime solitary
Profound sloping early
Fresh lustrous flurried
Brightened primal presiding
Flirtacious alive impassioned
Orange rose bluing
Charming delicate precocious
Natural sleeping standing
Embraced open reassembled
Shining discordant
Loose laughing enchanting
Sparkling resembling
Insensible secret subterranean
Sightless rude disastrous
Wooded grassy bloodstained
Savage obscure stammering
Sunny luminous
Flowery confused caressing
Instructed discreet ingenious
Faithful facile starry
Fleshy opaque throbbing
Unchanging contracted
Cobbled constructed vitrified
Global lofty popular
Barred guarded contradictory

Egale lourde métallique
Impitoyable impardonnable
Surprise dénouée rompue
Noire humiliée éclaboussée

Sommes-nous deux ou suis-je solitaire

Comme une femme solitaire
Qui dessine pour parler
Dans le désert
Et pour voir devant elle

L'année pourrait être heureuse
Un été en barres
Et l'hiver la neige est un lit bien fait
Quant au printemps on s'en détache
Avec des ailes bien formées

Revenue de la mort revenue de la vie
Je passe de juin à décembre
Par un miroir indifférent
Tout au creux de la vue

Comme une femme solitaire
Resterai-je ici-bas
Aurai-je un jour réponse à tout
Et réponse à personne

Le poids des murs ferme toutes les portes
Le poids des arbres épaissit la forêt
Va sur la pluie vers le ciel vertical
Rouge et semblable au sang qui noircira

Le soleil naît sur la tranche d'un fruit
La lune naît au sommet de mes seins
Le soleil fuit sur la rosée
La lune se limite

[1946]

Equal heavy metallic
Merciless pardonless
Surprised unraveled broken
Black humiliated bespattered

Are we two or am I all alone

Like a woman alone
Tracing pictures in order to speak
In the wilderness
And to see before her

The year might have been happy
One summer behind bars
In winter snow is a well-made bed
As for spring we free ourselves from it
With well-formed wings

Returned from death returned from life
I pass from June to December
By an indifferent mirror
In the shallow basin of sight

Like a woman alone
Shall I rest here below
Shall I have one day the answer to all
And an answer for no one

The weight of walls shuts all the gates
The weight of trees gives body to the forest
Goes above rain to the vertical sky
Red as the blood which will blacken

The sun is born on a slice of fruit
The moon is born at the summit of my breasts
The sunlight flees on the dew
The moon is bounded

La vérité c'est que j'aimais
Et la vérité c'est que j'aime
De jour en jour l'amour me prend première
Pas de regrets j'ignore tout d'hier
Je ne ferai pas de progrès

Sur une autre bouche
Le temps me prendrait première

Et l'amour n'a pas le temps
Qui dessine dans le sable
Sous la langue des grands vents

Je parle en l'air
A demi-mot
Je me comprends

L'aube et la bouche où rit l'azur des nuits
Pour un petit sourire tendre
Mon enfant frais de ce matin
Que personne ne regarde

Mon miroir est détaché
De la grappe des miroirs
Une maille détachée
L'amour juste le reprend

Rien ne peut déranger l'ordre de la lumière
Où je ne suis que moi-même
Et ce que j'aime
Et sur la table
Ce pot plein d'eau et le pain du repos
Au fil des mains drapées d'eau claire
Au fil du pain fait pour la main friande.
De l'eau fraîche et du pain chaud
Sur les deux versants du jour

The truth is that I loved
The truth is that I love
From day to day love takes me first
Without regret I know nothing of yesterday
I shall make no progress

On another mouth
Time would take me first

And love has not the time
Which traces in the sand
Beneath the tongues of mighty winds

I speak into the air
Half words
I understand myself

Dawn and the mouth where laughs the azure of the
      nights
For a tender little smile
My fresh child of this morning
That no one looks upon

My mirror is detached
From the cluster of mirrors
A stitch cut loose
And true love mends it

Nothing can disturb the order of the light
Where I am but myself
And what I love
And on the table
This cup of water and the bread of rest
With the thread of hands woven in clear water
With the thread of bread woven for the dainty
      hand
Cool water and warm bread
On both hillsides of the day

Aujourd'hui lumière unique
Aujourd'hui l'enfance entière
Changeant la vie en lumière
Sans passé sans lendemain
Aujourd'hui rêve de nuit
Au grand jour tout se délivre
Aujourd'hui je suis toujours

Je serai la première et la seule sans cesse
Il n'y a pas de drame il n'y a que mes yeux
Qu'un songe tient ouverts
Ma chair est ma vertu
Elle multiplie mon image

Je suis ma mère et mon enfant
En chaque point de l'éternel
Mon teint devient plus clair mon teint devient plus
        sombre
Je suis mon rayon de soleil
Et je suis mon bonheur nocturne

Tous les mots sont d'accord
La boue est caressante
Quand la terre dégèle
Le ciel est souterrain
Quand il montre la mort
Le soir est matinal
Après un jour de peine

Mais l'homme
L'homme aux lentes barbaries
L'homme comme un marais
L'homme à l'instinct brouillé
A la chair en exil
L'homme aux clartés de serre
Aux yeux fermés l'homme aux éclairs
L'homme mortel et divisé
Au front saignant d'espoir

Today unique light
Today entire childhood
Changing life to light
Without a past without a morrow
Today dream of night
In broad daylight all is freed
Today I am forever

I shall be the first the sole unceasing
There is no drama there are only my eyes
Held open by a dream
My flesh is my virtue
It multiplies my image

I am my mother and my child
In each point of the eternal
My complexion lightens my complexion darkens
I am my own ray of sunlight
I am my own noctural happiness

All words are in agreement
The mud is caressing
In a springtime thaw
The sky is underground
When it shows death
And evening is early
After a day of sorrow

But the man
Man of slow barbarities
Man like a marsh
Man of clouded instinct
Of flesh in exile
Man of a thousand windows
With closed eyes man of lightning
Man mortal and divided
With the forehead bleeding hope

L'homme en butte au passé
Et qui toujours regrette
Isolé quotidien
Dénué responsable

Savoir vieillir savoir passer le temps

Savoir régner savoir durer savoir revivre
Il rejeta ses draps il éclaira sa chambre
Il ouvrit les miroirs légers de sa jeunesse
Et les longues allées qui l'avaient reconduit

Etre un enfant être une plume à sa naissance
Etre la source invariable et transparente
Toujours être au cœur blanc une goutte de sang
Une goutte de feu toujours renouvelée

Mordre un rire innocent mordre à même la vie
Rien n'a changé candeur rien n'a changé désir
L'hiver j'ai mon soleil il fait fleurir ma neige
Et l'été qui sent bon à toutes les faiblesses

L'on m'aimera car j'aime par-dessus tout ordre
Et je suis prêt à tout pour l'avenir de tous
Et je ne connais rien de rien à l'avenir
Mais j'aime pour aimer et je mourrai d'amour

Il se mit à genoux pour un premier baiser
La nuit était pareille à la nuit d'autrefois
Et ce fut le départ et la fin du passé
La conscience amère qu'il avait vécu

Man on the hillock of the past
Who always regrets
Isolated everyday
Destitute responsible

To know how to grow old to know how to pass the
    time

To know how to rule to endure now to live again
He threw back the sheets lit the lamp of the
    chamber
He opened the light mirrors of his youth
And the long paths which had brought him back
    to it

To be a child to be a feather at its birth
To be the invariable and transparent source
Always to be a drop of blood on a white heart
A drop of fire always renewed

To bite innocent laughter even to bite a life
Nothing has changed candor nothing has changed
    desire
In winter I have my sunlight it makes my snow
    blossom
And summer that smells good to all frailties

I shall be loved for I love above all order
I am ready for all for the future of all
I know nothing of anything in the future
But I love for the sake of loving and I shall die of
    love

He fell on his knees for one first kiss
Night like the night of another time
This was the parting the finish of the past
The bitter conscience he had lived

Alors il réveilla les ombres endormies
La cendre grise et froide d'un murmure tu
La cendre de l'aveugle et la stérilité
Le jour sans espérance et la nuit sans sommeil

L'égale pauvreté d'une vie limitée

Tous les mots se reflètent
Et les larmes aussi
Dans la force perdue
Dans la force rêvée

Hier c'est la jeunesse hier c'est la promesse

Pour qu'un seul baiser la retienne
Pour que l'entoure le plaisir
Comme un été blanc bleu et blanc
Pour qu'il lui soit règle d'or pur
Pour que sa gorge bouge douce
Sous la chaleur tirant la chair
Vers une caresse infinie
Pour qu'elle soit comme une plaine
Nue et visible de partout
Pour qu'elle soit comme une pluie
Miraculeuse sans nuage
Comme une pluie entre deux feux
Comme une larme entre deux rires
Pour qu'elle soit neige bénie
Sous l'aile tiède d'un oiseau
Lorsque le sang coule plus vite
Dans les veines du vent nouveau
Pour que ses paupières ouvertes
Approfondissent la lumière
Parfum total à son image
Pour que sa bouche et le silence
Intelligibles se comprennent
Pour que ses mains posent leur paume

[1946]

Then he awakened the sleeping shadows
The cold grey ashes of a silent murmur
The ash of blindness and sterility
The day without hope and the night without
    slumber

The even poverty of a bounded life

All words are reflected
And the tears as well
In the lost strength
In the dreamed-of strength

Yesterday is youth yesterday is promise

To let one kiss keep her
To let pleasure surround her
Like summer white blue and white
A measure of pure gold for her
To let her throat move sweetly
Under the warmth drawing the flesh
To an infinite caress
To let her be like a plain
Naked visible from everywhere
To let her be like a rainfall
Miraculous and cloudless
Like rain between two fires
Like a tear between two laughs
To let her be blessed snow
Beneath a bird's warm wing
When the blood flows faster
In the veins of a new wind
To let her opened eyelids
Dive deep into the light
The total perfume in her image
To let her lips and silence
Intelligible understand each other
To let her hands rest their palms

169

Sur chaque tête qui s'éveille
Pour que les lignes de ses mains
Se continuent dans d'autres mains
Distances à passer le temps

Je fortifierai mon délire

De l'océan à la source
De la montagne à la plaine
Court le fantôme de la vie
L'ombre sordide de la mort
Mais entre nous
Une aube naît de chair ardente
Et bien précise
Qui remet la terre en état
Nous avançons d'un pas tranquille
Et la nature nous salue
Le jour incarne nos couleurs
Le feu nos yeux et la mer notre union

Et tous les vivants nous ressemblent
Tous les vivants que nous aimons

Les autres sont imaginaires
Faux et cernés de leur néant
Mais il nous faut lutter contre eux
Ils vivent à coups de poignard
Ils parlent comme un meuble craque
Leurs lèvres tremblent de plaisir
A l'écho des cloches de plomb
A la mutité d'un or noir

Un cœur seul pas de cœur
Un seul cœur tous les cœurs
Et les corps chaque étoile
Dans un ciel plein d'étoiles
Dans la carrière en mouvement

On every wakening head
To let the lines of her hands
Continue in other hands
Distances to pass the time

I shall fortify my frenzy

From the ocean to the source
From the mountain to the plain
Races the phantom of life
Sordid shadow of death
But between us
A dawn is born of ardent flesh
Of exact flesh
That puts the earth in order
We advance with tranquil step
And nature does us homage
The day embodies our colors
The flame our eyes the sea our union

And all the living resemble us
All the living whom we love

The others are imaginary
False and encircled with their nothingness
But we must fight against them
They live by dagger thrusts
They speak as a chair cracks
Their lips tremble with pleasure
At the echo of leaden bells
At the muteness of a black gold

One heart alone no heart
One whole heart all hearts
And the bodies every star
In a star-filled sky
In the moving course

De la lumière et des regards
Notre poids brillant sur terre
Patine de la volupté

A chanter des plages humaines
Pour toi la vivante que j'aime
Et pour tous ceux que nous aimons
Qui n'ont envie que de s'aimer
Je finirai bien par barrer la route
Au flot des rêves imposés
Je finirai bien par me retrouver
Nous prendrons possession du monde

O rire végétal ouvrant une clairière
De gorges chantonnant interminablement
Mains où le sang s'est effacé
Où l'innocence est volontaire
Gaieté gagnée tendresse du bois mort
Chaleurs d'hiver pulpes séchées
Fraîcheurs d'été sortant des fleurs nouvelles
Constant amour multiplié tout nu

Rien à haïr et rien à pardonner
Aucun destin n'illustre notre front
Dans l'orage notre faiblesse
Est l'aiguille la plus sensible
Et la raison de l'orage
Image ô contact parfait
L'espace est notre milieu
Et le temps notre horizon

Quelques cailloux sur un sentier battu
De l'herbe comme un souvenir vague
Le ciel couvert et la nuit en avance
Quelques vitrines étrennant leurs lampes
Des trous la porte et la fenêtre ouvertes
Sur des gens qui sont enfermés

172

Of light and looks
Our weight brilliant on earth
Patina of voluptuousness

To sing the human seacoasts
For you the living woman whom I love
And for all those we love
Who want only to love
I shall end by blocking off the road
Against the flood of self-inflicted dreams
I shall end by finding myself again
And we shall take possession of the world

O vegetal laugh opening a clearing
Of throats humming interminably
Hands where blood is obliterated
Where innocence is voluntary
Gaiety won over tenderness of dead wood
Heat of winter dried-out pulps
Coolness of summer springing from new flowers
Constant love multiplied all naked

Nothing to hate and nothing to pardon
No destiny shines on our forehead
In the tempest our frailty
Is the most sensitive needle
And the reason of the tempest
Image O perfect contact
Space is our center
And time our horizon

A few pebbles on a beaten pathway
Of grass like a vague memory
The sky cloudy night advancing
A few windows trying out their lamps
Of holes the door and window open
On men who are locked in

Un petit bar vendu et revendu
Apothéose de chiffres
Et de soucis et de mains sales

Un désastre profond
Où tout est mesuré même la tristesse
Même la dérision
Même la honte
La plainte est inutile
Le rire est imbécile
Le désert des taches grandit
Mieux que sur un suaire

Les yeux ont disparu les oiseaux volent bas
On n'entend plus le bruit des pas
Le silence est comme une boue
Pour les projets sans lendemain
Et soudain un enfant crie
Dans la cage de son ennui
Un enfant remue des cendres
Et rien de vivant ne bouge

Je rends compte du réel
Je prends garde à mes paroles
Je ne veux pas me tromper
Je veux savoir d'où je pars
Pour conserver tant d'espoir

Mes origines sont les larmes
Et la fatigue et la douleur
Et le moins de beauté
Et le moins de bonté

Le regret d'être au monde et l'amour sans vertu
M'ont enfanté dans la misère
Comme un murmure comme une ombre

174

[1946]

A little bar sold and sold again
Apotheosis of ciphers
Of care and of dirty hands

A profound disaster
Where all is measured even sadness
Even derision
Even shame
Complaint is useless
Laughter is imbecile
The wilderness of stains grows great
Better than on a shroud

The eyes have disappeared the birds fly low
The sound of footsteps is heard no longer
Silence is like a mire
For plans without a morrow
And suddenly a child cries
In the cage of his weariness
A child stirs the ashes
And nothing living moves

I record reality
I watch my words closely
I want to make no mistake
I want to know from where I leave
To conserve so much hope

My origins are tears
Fatigue and sorrow
And the least of beauty
And the least of goodness

The regret of being in the world and love without
    virtue
Gave birth to me in misery
As a murmur as a shadow

Ils mourront ils sont morts
Mais ils vivront glorieux
Sable dans le cristal
Nourricier malgré lui
Plus clair qu'en plein soleil

Le regret d'être au monde

Je n'ai pas de regrets
Plus noir plus lourd est mon passé
Plus léger et limpide est l'enfant que j'étais
L'enfant que je serai
Et la femme que je protège
La femme dont j'assume
L'éternelle confiance

Comme une femme solitaire
Qui dessine pour parler
Dans le désert
Et pour voir devant elle
Par charmes et caprices
Par promesses par abandons

Entr'ouverte à la vie
Toujours soulignée de bleu

Comme une femme solitaire
A force d'être l'une ou l'autre
Et tous les éléments

Je saurai dessiner comme mes mains épousent
La forme de mon corps
Je saurai dessiner comme le jour pénètre
Au fin fond de mes yeux

176

[1946]

They shall die they are dead
But they shall live gloriously
Sand in the crystal
Nourishing in spite of itself
Brighter than broad daylight

The regret of being in the world

I have no regrets
Blacker and heavier is my past
Lighter and more limpid is the child I was
The child that I shall be
And the woman I protect
The woman of whom I assume
Eternal confidence

Like a woman alone
Tracing pictures in order to speak
In the wilderness
And to see before her
By charm and caprice
By promise and abandon

Half opened to life
Forever underlined in blue

Like a woman alone
By dint of being one or the other
And all the elements

I shall know how to trace as my hands wed
The form of my body
I shall know how to trace as light penetrates
The fine foundation of my eyes

Et ma chaleur fera s'étendre les couleurs
Sur le lit de mes nuits
Sur la nature nue où je tiens une place
Plus grande que mes songes

Où je suis seule et nue où je suis l'absolu
L'être définitif

La première femme apparue
Le premier homme rencontré
Sortant du jeu qui les mêlait
Comme doigts d'une même main

La première femme étrangère
Et le premier homme inconnu
La première douleur exquise
Et le premier plaisir panique

Et la première différence
Entre des êtres fraternels
Et la première ressemblance
Entre des êtres différents

Le premier champ de neige vierge
Pour un enfant né en été
Le premier lait entre les lèvres
D'un fils de chair de sang secret

Buisson de roses et d'épines
Route de terre et de cailloux
A ciel ardent ciel consumé
A froid intense tête claire

Rocher de fardeaux et d'épaules
Lac de reflets et de poissons
A jour mauvais bonté remise
A mer immense voile lourde

And my warmth will make the colors spread
On the bed of my nights
On naked nature where I hold a place
Much greater than my dreams

Where I am alone and naked where I am the
    absolute
The definitive being

The first woman to appear
The first man met
Springing from the game which mingled them
Like fingers on the same hand

The first strange woman
And the first unknown man
The first exquisite pain
And the first panic pleasure

And the first difference
Between fraternal beings
And the first resemblance
Between different beings

The first field of virgin snow
For a child born in summer
The first milk between the lips
Of a child of flesh of secret blood

Bush of roses and thorns
Road of earth and pebbles
Of ardent sky consumed sky
Of intense cold the head clear

Crag of burdens and shoulders
Lake of reflections and fish
Goodness set back to a bad day
The heavy sail of an immense sea

Et j'écris pour marquer les années et les jours
Les heures et les hommes leur durée
Et les parties d'un corps commun
Qui a son matin
Et son midi et son minuit
Et de nouveau son matin
Inévitable et paré
De force et de faiblesse
De beauté de laideur
De repos agréable et de misérable lumière
Et de gloire provoquée

D'un matin sorti d'un rêve le pouvoir
De mener à bien la vie
Les matins passés les matins futurs
Et d'organiser le désastre
Et de séparer la cendre du feu

D'une maison les lumières naturelles
Et les ponts jetés sur l'aube
D'un matin la chair nouvelle
La chair intacte pétrie d'espoir
Dans la maison comme un glaçon qui fond

Du bonheur la vue sans pitié
Les yeux bien plantés sur leurs jambes
Dans la fumée de la santé
Du bonheur comme une règle
Comme un couteau impitoyable
Tranchant de tout
Sauf de la nécessité

D'une famille le cœur clos
Gravé d'un nom insignifiant

And I write to mark the years and days
The hours the men and their duration
And the parts of a common body
Which has its morning
Noon and midnight
And again its morning
Inevitable and adorned
With strength and weakness
With beauty and ugliness
With pleasant rest and wretched light
With challenged glory

The power of a morning come from a dream
To lead a life of goodness
The mornings past the future mornings
To organize disaster
To separate the ashes from the fire

The natural lights of a house
And bridges thrown across the dawn
The new flesh of a morning
The flesh intact kneaded by hope
In the house like a melting icicle

The pitiless sight of happiness
The eyes well planted on their legs
In the smoke of health
Happiness like a measure
Like a merciless knife
Cutting all
Except necessity

The closed heart of a family
Engraved with an insignificant name

D'un rire la vertu comme un jeu sans perdants
Montagne et plaine
Calculées en tout point
Un cadeau contre un cadeau
Béatitudes s'annulant

D'un brasier les cloches d'or aux paupières lentes
Sur un paysage sans fin
Volière peinte dans l'azur
Et d'un sein supposé le poids sans réserves
Et d'un ventre accueillant la pensée sans raison
Et d'un brasier les cloches d'or aux yeux profonds
Dans un visage grave et pur

D'une volière peinte en bleu
Où les oiseaux sont des épis
Jetant leur or aux pauvres
Pour plus vite entrer dans le noir
Dans le silence hivernal

D'une rue
D'une rue ma défiguration
Au profit de tous et de toutes
Les inconnus dans la poussière
Ma solitude mon absence

D'une rue sans suite
Et sans saluts
Vitale
Et pourtant épuisante
La rencontre niée

De la fatigue le brouillard
Prolonge loques et misères
A l'intérieur de la poitrine
Et le vide aux tempes éteintes
Et le crépuscule aux artères

182

The virtue of laughter like a game without losers
Mountain and plain
Calculated on every point
A gift for a gift
Blessings canceled out

The golden bells with slow eyelids of a clear fire
On an endless countryside
A birdhouse painted in the sky
The weight without reserve of a supposed breast
Of a womb welcoming thought without reason
The golden bells with profound eyes of a clear fire
In a face grave and pure

Of a birdhouse painted blue
Where the birds are spikes of wheat
Casting their gold to the poor
The quicker to enter the darkness
In winter silence

Of a street
My disfiguration of a street
For the profit of all men and women
The unknowns in the dust
My solitude my absence

Of a street without issue
Without greeting
Vital
And yet exhausting
The meeting denied

The fog of weariness
Prolongs rags and miseries
Within the breast
And the void with extinguished temples
And the arteried twilight

Du bonheur la vue chimérique
Comme au bord d'un abîme
Quand une grosse bulle blanche
Vous crève dans la tête
Et que le cœur est inutilement libre
Mais du bonheur promis et qui commence à deux
La première parole
Est déjà un refrain confiant
Contre la peur contre la faim
Un signe de ralliement

D'une main composée pour moi
Et qu'elle soit faible qu'importe
Cette main double la mienne
Pour tout lier tout délivrer
Pour m'endormir pour m'éveiller

D'un baiser la nuit des grands rapports humains
Un corps auprès d'un autre corps
La nuit des grands rapports terrestres
La nuit native de ta bouche
La nuit où rien ne se sépare

Que ma parole pèse sur la nuit qui passe
Et que s'ouvre toujours la porte par laquelle
Tu es entrée dans ce poème
Porte de ton sourire et porte de ton corps

Par toi je vais de la lumière à la lumière
De la chaleur à la chaleur
C'est par toi que je parle et tu restes au centre
De tout comme un soleil consentant au bonheur

Mais il nous faut encore un peu
Accorder nos yeux clairs à ces nuits inhumaines
Des hommes qui n'ont pas trouvé la vie sur terre
Il nous faut qualifier leur sort pour les sauver

The phantom sight of happiness
As on the brink of an abyss
When a great white bubble
Breaks within your head
And the heart is uselessly free
But of promised happiness which begins by two
The first word
Already a confident refrain
Against fear against famine
A sign of rallying

Of a hand composed for me
If it be weak what matter
This hand lines my own
To bind all to deliver all
To cradle me in sleep to wake me

The night of great human affinities of a kiss
One body near another body
The night of great earthly affinities
And your mouth's native night
The night where nothing is separate

May my word weigh on the passing night
And may the door be ever open
By which you entered in this poem
Door of your smile your body's door

Through you I go from light to light
From warmth to warmth
I speak through you and you stay at the center
Of all like a sun consenting to happiness

But we need a little more
To reconcile our clear eyes to these inhuman nights
Of men who have not found a life on earth
We must qualify their fate to save them

Nous partirons d'en bas nous partirons d'en haut
De la tête trop grosse et de la tête infime
En haut un rien de tête en bas l'enflure ignoble
En haut rien que du front en bas rien que menton
Rien que prison collant aux os
Rien que chair vague et que poisons gobés
Par la beauté par la laideur sans répugnance
Toujours un œil aveugle une langue muette
Une main inutile un cœur sans résonance
Près d'une langue experte et qui voit loin
Près d'un œil éloquent près d'une main prodigue
Trop près d'un cœur qui fait la loi

La loi la feuille morte et la voile tombée
La loi la lampe éteinte et le plaisir gâché
La nourriture sacrifiée l'amour absurde
La neige sale et l'aile inerte et la vieillesse

Sur les champs un ciel étroit
Soc du néant sur les tombes

Au tournant les chiens hurlant
Vers une carcasse folle

Au tournant l'eau est crêpue
Et les champs claquent des dents

Et les chiens sont des torchons
Léchant des vitres brisées

Sur les champs la puanteur
Roule noire et bien musclée

Sur le ciel tout ébréché
Les étoiles sont moisies

186

We shall start from below we shall start from above
From the head too thick and the head too mean
Above a nothingness of head below the ignoble
    swelling
Above nothing but forehead below nothing but chin
Nothing but prisons clinging to the bones
Nothing but vague flesh and poison swallowed
By beauty by ugliness without repugnance
Always a blind eye always a muted tongue
A useless hand a heart without resonance
Near an expert far-seeing tongue
Near an eloquent eye near a prodigal hand
Too near a heart which makes the law

The law the dead leaf the law the fallen sail
The law the burnt-out lamp and the spoiled pleasure
Sacrificed nourishment and absurd love
The dirty snow the inert wing and old age

Above the fields a narrow sky
Plowshare of nothingness above the tombs

At the turn dogs howl
About a maddened carcass

At the turn the water is crinkled
And the fields' teeth chatter

And the dogs are rags
Licking the broken windows

Over the fields the stench
Rolls black and muscular

The stars are moldy
In a jagged sky

Allez donc penser à l'homme
Allez donc faire un enfant

Allez donc pleurer ou rire
Dans ce monde de buvard

Prendre forme dans l'informe
Prendre empreinte dans le flou

Prendre sens dans l'insensé
Dans ce monde sans espoir

Si nous montions d'un degré

Le jour coule comme un œuf
Le vent fané s'effiloche

Toute victoire est semblable
Des ennemis des amis

Ennemis amis pâlots
Que même le repos blesse

Et de leurs drapeaux passés
Ils enveloppent leurs crampes

Beaux oiseaux évaporés
Ils rêvent de leurs pensées

Ils se tissent des chapeaux
Cent fois plus grands que leur tête

Ils méditent leur absence
Et se cachent dans leur ombre

Ils ont été au présent
Ceci entre parenthèses

Go think about man
Go make a child

Go weep or laugh
In this blotter world

Take form within the formless
Take imprint in the foam

Make sense in madness
In this hopeless world

If we go up one degree

The day flows like an egg
The faded wind unravels

All victory is alike
Enemies like friends

Pallid enemies and friends
Wounded even by repose

And in their faded banners
They wind their cramps

Beautiful evaporated birds
They dream of their thoughts

They weave themselves hats
A hundred times larger than their heads

They meditate their absence
And hide in their own shadow

They have been in the present
This between parentheses

Ils croient qu'ils ont été des diables des lionceaux
Des chasseurs vigoureux des nègres transparents
Des intrus sans vergogne et des rustres impurs
Des monstres opalins et des zèbres pas mal

Des anonymes redoutables
Des calembours et des charades

Et la ligne de flottaison
Sur le fleuve héraclitéen

Et l'hospitalité amère
Dans un asile carnassier

Et le déshonneur familial
Et le point sec des abreuvoirs

Ils croient ils croient mais entre nous
Il vaut encore mieux qu'ils croient

Si nous montions d'un degré

C'est la santé l'élégance
En dessous roses et noirs

Rousseurs chaudes blancheurs sobres
Rien de gros rien de brumeux

Les coquilles dans la nuit
D'un piano sans fondations

Les voitures confortables
Aux roues comme des guirlandes

C'est le luxe des bagages
Blasés jetés à la mer

They believe they have been devils lion-cubs
Mighty hunters transparent negroes
Shameless intruders and impure clowns
Opaline monsters and fairly decent zebras

Redoubtable anonyms
Puns and charades

The high water mark
On the Heraclitean river

And the bitter hospitality
In the wild beasts' den

And the family dishonor
The drypoint of the horsetroughs

They believe they believe but between us
It were better if they did believe

If we go up one degree

It is health and elegance
In pink and black underclothes

Hot redness sober whiteness
Nothing gross nothing foggy

Shells in the night
Of a bottomless piano

Comfortable carriages
With wheels like garlands

This is the luxury of baggage
Indifferent cast into the sea

Et l'aisance du language
Digéré comme un clou par un mur

Les idées à la rigolade
Les désirs à l'office

Une poule un vin la merde
Réchauffés entretenus

Si nous montions d'un degré
Dans ce monde sans images

Vers la plainte d'un berger
Qui est seul et qui a froid

Vers une main généreuse
Qui se tend et que l'on souille

Vers un aveugle humilié
De se cogner aux fenêtres

Vers l'excuse désolée
D'un malheureux sans excuses

Vers le bavardage bête
Des victimes consolées

Semaines dimanches lâches
Qui s'épanchent dans le vide

Durs travaux loisirs gâchés
Peaux grises résorbant l'homme

Moralité de fourmi
Sous les pieds d'un plus petit

Si nous montions d'un degré

And the ease of language
Digested like a nail by a wall

Ideas in bursts of laughter
Desires in servant's quarters

A skirt a glass of wine a turd
Warmed over kept up

If we go up one degree
In this world without images

To the complaint of a shepherd
Cold and alone

To a generous hand
Extended and spat upon

To a blindman humiliated
By stumbling against windows

To the desolate excuse
Of a wretch without excuses

To the stupid chatter
Of consoled victims

Weeks cowardly Sundays
That pour themselves into a void

Hard labor spoiled leisure
Grey skins absorbing man

The ant's morality
Under the feet of a smaller one

If we go up one degree

La misère s'éternise
La cruauté s'assouvit

Les guerres s'immobilisent
Sur les glaciers opulents

Entre les armes en broussailles
Sèchent la viande et le sang

De quoi calmer les âmes amoureuses
De quoi varier le cours des rêveries

De quoi provoquer l'oubli
Aussi de quoi changer la loi

La loi la raison pratique

Et que comprendre juge
L'erreur selon l'erreur

Si voir était la foudre
Au pays des charognes

Le juge serait dieu
Il n'y a pas de dieu

Si nous montions d'un degré

Vers l'extase sans racines
Toute bleue j'en suis payé

Aussi bien que de cantiques
Et de marches militaires

Et de mots définitifs
Et de bravos entraînants

194

Misery becomes eternal
Cruelty gluts itself

Wars immobilise themselves
On opulent glaciers

Meat and blood parch
Between brushwood weapons

The wherewithal to calm the amorous souls
The wherewithal to change the course of reveries

The wherewithal to breed oblivion
Also the wherewithal to change the law

The law the practical reason

Let understanding judge
Error according to error

If seeing were the lightning
In the land of carrion

The judge would be god
There is no god

If we go up one degree

To a rootless ecstasy
All blue I'm paid by it

As well as canticles
And military marches

And definitive words
And captivating bravos

Et la secousse idéale
De la vanité sauvage

Et le bruit insupportable
Des objecteurs adaptés

Le golfe d'une serrure
Abrite trop de calculs

Et je tremble comme un arbre
Au passage des saisons

Ma sève n'est qu'une excuse
Mon sang n'est qu'une raison

Si nous montions d'un degré

Mes vieux amis mon vieux Paul
Il faut avouer

Tout avouer et non seulement le désespoir
Vice des faibles sans sommeil

Et pas seulement nos rêves
Vertu des forts anéantis

Mais le reflet brouillé la vilaine blessure
Du voyant dénaturé

Vous acceptez j'accepte d'être infirme
La même sueur baigne notre suicide

Mes vieux amis

Vieux innocents et vieux coupables
Dressés contre la solitude

[1946]

And the ideal shock
Of savage vanity

And the intolerable noise
Of adapted objectors

The gulf of a lock
Shelters too much calculation

And I tremble like a tree
At the passage of the seasons

My sap is only an excuse
My blood is but a reason

If we go up one degree

My old friends my old Paul
We must confess

Confess all not only despair
Vice of the sleepless weak

And not our dreams alone
Virtue of destroyed strong-men

But the clouded reflection and the ugly wound
Of the denatured prophet

You accept I accept infirmity
The same sweat bathes our suicide

My old friends

Old innocent old guilty
Trained against solitude

Où s'allume notre folie
Où s'accuse notre impatience

Nous ne sommes seuls qu'ensemble
Nos amours se contredisent

Nous exigeons tout de rien
L'exception devient banale

Mais notre douleur aussi
Et notre déchéance

Nous nous réveillons impurs
Nous nous révélons obscurs

Brutes mentales du chaos
Vapeurs uniques de l'abîme

Dans la basse région lyrique
Où nous nous sommes réunis

Mes vieux amis pour être séparés
Pour être plus nombreux

Si nous montions d'un degré

Sur des filles couronnées
Une épave prend le large

A l'orient de mon destin
Aurai-je un frère demain

Sur des ruines virginales
Aux ailes de papillon

Friandises de l'hiver
Quand la mère joue la morte

Where our folly lights itself
Where our impatience accuses itself

We are alone only together
Our loves contradict themselves

We demand all from nothing
The exception becomes commonplace

But our sorrow too
Our decadence as well

We awake impure
We show ourselves obscure

Mental brutes of chaos
Unique vapors of the abyss

In the low lyric region
Where we have joined together

My old friends in order to be separate
To be more numerous

If we go up one degree

On crowned maidens
A derelict drifts out to sea

To the orient of my destiny
Will I have a brother tomorrow

On virginal ruins
With butterfly's wings

Sweetmeats of winter
When the mother plays dead

Sans passion et sans dégoût
Une ruche couve lourde
Dans une poche gluante

Paume attachée à son bien
Comme la cruche à son eau
Et le printemps aux bourgeons

Fer épousé par la forge
Or maté en chambre forte

Nue inverse rocher souple
D'où rebondit la cascade

Simulacre du sein
Livré aux égoïstes

Mais aussi le sein offert
De l'image reconquise

Plaisir complet plaisir austère
Pommier noir aux pommes mûres

Belle belle rôde et jouit
Fluorescente dentelle

Où l'éclair est une aiguille
La pluie le fil

L'aile gauche du cœur
Se replie sur le cœur

Je vois brûler l'eau pure et l'herbe du matin
Je vais de fleur en fleur sur un corps auroral
Midi qui dort je veux l'entourer de clameurs
L'honorer dans son jour de senteurs de lueurs

Without passion and without revulsion
A hive broods heavy
In a sticky pocket

Palm attached to its goods
As the pitcher to its water
As springtime to its buds

Iron wedded by the forge
Gold dulled in a crucible

Inverse cloud and supple cliff
From whence the waterfall leaps back

The image of a breast
Given to egotists

But as well the proffered breast
Of the reconquered image

Complete pleasure austere pleasure
Black appletree with ripe apples

Beautiful lovely roving and enjoying
The fluorescent lace

Where lightning is a needle
And rain the thread

The left wing of the heart
Folds back upon the heart

I see pure water burning and the morning grass
I go from flower to flower on daybreak's body
And sleeping noon I will surround with outcries
Honor it in its day of perfumes of soft light

Je ne me méfie plus je suis un fils de femme
La vacance de l'homme et le temps bonifié
La réplique grandiloquente
Des étoiles minuscules

Et nous montons

Les derniers arguments du néant sont vaincus
Et le dernier bourdonnement
Des pas revenant sur eux-mêmes

Peu à peu se décomposent
Les alphabets ânonnés
De l'histoire et des morales
Et la syntaxe soumise
Des souvenirs enseignés

Et c'est très vite
La liberté conquise
La liberté feuille de mai
Chauffée à blanc
Et le feu aux nuages
Et le feu aux oiseaux
Et le feu dans les caves
Et les hommes dehors
Et les hommes partout
Tenant toute la place
Abattant les murailles

Se partageant le pain
Dévêtant le soleil
S'embrassant sur le front
Habillant les orages
Et s'embrassant les mains
Faisant fleurir charnel
Et le temps et l'espace

[1946]

I distrust myself no longer I am the son of woman
The vacancy of man and time made good
The grandiloquent reply
Of microscopic stars

And we go higher

The last arguments of nothingness are conquered
And the final buzzing
Of steps returning on themselves

Little by little are decomposed
The stammering alphabets
Of history of morals
And the submissive syntax
Of learned memories

And it's very quick
Liberty conquered
May-leaf liberty
Heated white
The fire in the clouds
The fire in the birds
The fire in the cellars
And the men outside
And the men everywhere
Holding all places
Breaking down the walls

Sharing the bread
Unveiling the sun
Kissing on the forehead
Dressing the tempests
Kissing hands
Making flesh flower
And time and space

Faisant chanter les verrous
Et respirer les poitrines

Les prunelles s'écarquillent
Les cachettes se dévoilent
La pauvreté rit aux larmes
De ses chagrins ridicules
Et minuit mûrit des fruits
Et midi mûrit des lunes

Tout se vide et se remplit
Au rythme de l'infini
Et disons la vérité
La jeunesse est un trésor
La vieillesse est un trésor
L'océan est un trésor
Et la terre est une mine
L'hiver est une fourrure
L'été une boisson fraîche
Et l'automne un lait d'accueil

Quant au printemps c'est l'aube
Et la bouche c'est l'aube
Et les yeux immortels
Ont la forme de tout

Nous deux toi toute nue
Moi tel que j'ai vécu

Toi la source du sang
Et moi les mains ouvertes
Comme des yeux

Nous deux nous ne vivons que pour être fidèles
A la vie
. . . .

Making the bolts sing
Making the breasts breathe

The eyes open wider
The hidden places are revealed
Poverty laughs to tears
At its ridiculous dismay
And midnight ripens fruit
And mid-day ripens moons

All empties and refills
In the rhythm of the infinite
And let us tell the truth
Youth is a treasure
Old age is a treasure
The ocean is a treasure
The earth is a full mine
Winter is a fine fur
Summer a cooling drink
Autumn the milk of welcome

And springtime is the dawn
And the mouth is the dawn
And the immortal eyes
Have the form of all

We two and you all naked
Myself such as I have lived

You the fountainhead of blood
I with my hands open
Like eyes

And we two we live only to be faithful
To life
. . . .

EN ESPAGNE

S'il y a en Espagne un arbre teint de sang
C'est l'arbre de la liberté

S'il y a en Espagne une bouche bavarde
Elle parle de liberté

S'il y a en Espagne un verre de vin pur
C'est le peuple qui le boira.

⊙

ESPAGNE

Les plus beaux yeux du monde
Se sont mis à chanter
Qu'ils veulent voir plus loin
Que les murs des prisons
Plus loin que leurs paupières
Meurtries par le chagrin

Les barreaux de la cage
Chantent la liberté
Un air qui prend le large
Sur les routes humaines
Sous un soleil furieux
Un grand soleil d'orage

Vie perdue retrouvée
Nuit et jour de la vie
Exilés prisonniers
Vous nourrissez dans l'ombre
Un feu qui porte l'aube
La fraîcheur la rosée

IN SPAIN

If there is one bloodstained tree in Spain
It is the tree of liberty

If there is one talkative mouth in Spain
It speaks of liberty

If there is one glass of pure wine in Spain
The people will drink it.

⊙

SPAIN

The most beautiful eyes in the world
Began to sing
That they must see farther
Than the walls of prisons
Farther than their eyelids
Wounded by dismay

The very bars of the cage
Sing liberty
An air which carries
Over all human roads
Under a furious sun
A great sun of tempest

Life lost and found again
Night and day of life
Exiles prisoners
In darkness you feed
A fire bearing dawn
Freshness dew

La victoire

Et le plaisir de la victoire.

⊙

VENCER JUNTOS

Ici la vie est limitée
Par cette ligne de sang noir
Qui nous sépare
Des prisons et des tombeaux

Ici nous sommes rabaissés
Par le supplice de l'Espagne
Ici la vie est menacée
Par la frontière de l'Espagne

Mais que l'Espagne crie victoire
Et notre sang deviendra chair
Chair confondue et chair heureuse
La France aura gagné sa guerre.

⊙

« LA POESIE DOIT AVOIR POUR BUT LA VERITE PRATIQUE »

A mes amis exigeants

Si je vous dis que le soleil dans la forêt
Est comme un ventre qui se donne dans un lit
Vous me croyez vous approuvez tous mes désirs

[1948]

Victory

And the pleasure of victory.

⊙

VENCER JUNTOS

Here life is limited
By this line of black blood
Which separates us
From the prisons and the graves

Here we are humiliated
By the torture of Spain
Here life is threatened
By the frontier of Spain

But once let Spain cry victory
And our blood will turn to flesh
United happy flesh
France will have won her war.

⊙

« POETRY MUST HAVE
PRACTICAL TRUTH AS ITS GOAL »

To my exacting friends

If I tell you that sunlight in the forest
Is like a passionate belly in a bed
You believe me you approve all my desires

Si je vous dis que le cristal d'un jour de pluie
Sonne toujours dans la paresse de l'amour
Vous me croyez vous allongez le temps d'aimer

Si je vous dis que sur les branches de mon lit
Fait son nid un oiseau qui ne dit jamais oui
Vous me croyez vous partagez mon inquiétude

Si je vous dis que dans le golfe d'une source
Tourne la clé d'un fleuve entr'ouvrant la verdure
Vous me croyez encore plus vous me comprenez

Mais si je chante sans détours ma rue entière
Et mon pays entier comme une rue sans fin
Vous ne me croyez plus vous allez au désert

Car vous marchez sans but sans savoir que les
    hommes
Ont besoin d'être unis d'espérer de lutter
Pour expliquer le monde et pour le transformer

D'un seul pas de mon cœur je vous entraînerai
Je suis sans forces j'ai vécu je vis encore
Mais je m'étonne de parler pour vous ravir
Quand je voudrais vous libérer pour vous confondre
Aussi bien avec l'algue et le jonc de l'aurore
Qu'avec nos frères qui construisent leur lumière.

⊙

APRES TANT D'ANNEES

Après tant d'années passées à souffrir
Tant d'années-poussière au souffle plus long
Qu'années-lumière vers un astre disparu
Nous retrouvons misère à vendre et à revendre
Pour rien et rien n'est pas un mot pour nous

210

[1948]

If I tell you that the sparkle of a rainy day
Forever rings throughout the indolence of love
You believe me you draw out the time for loving

If I tell you that in the branches of my bed
Nests a bird which never says yes
You believe me you share my distress

If I tell you that in the gulf of a spring
Turns the key of a river opening verdure
You believe me even more you understand

But if I sing my whole road without a turning
And my whole country like an endless street
You believe me no longer you go to the wilderness

For you wander aimlessly without knowing that
     men
Need unity need hope and struggle
To explain the world and change it

With a single step of my heart I shall lead you
I am without strength I have lived I am still alive
But I am astonished speaking only to delight you
When I would free you to unite you
As well with algae and the reeds of dawn
As with our brothers building their own daylight.

☉

AFTER SO MANY YEARS

After so many years spent in suffering
So many dust-years with breath longer
Than light-years to a vanished star
Once more we find misery enough to sell and sell
     again
For nothing and nothing is not a word for us

Notre combat notre travail font-ils faillite
Le désespoir s'est-il couché dans notre lit
Nous rêvions d'embrasser la santé la jeunesse
Sur la bouche et le front nous en rêvons encore
Notre vie changera comme change un enfant

Nous n'avons pas désespéré nous survivons
Tout a été plus dur plus obscur que jamais
Mais la nuit ne s'est pas mêlée à notre sang
Un pas de plus ensemble et le sentier se rompt
Pour nous offrir à tous notre bien notre route.

☉

DANS VARSOVIE

LA VILLE FANTASTIQUE

Qui n'a pas vu les ruines du Ghetto
Ne connaît pas le destin de son corps
Quand mort le fête et que son cœur pourrit
Quand son unique absence fait le vide

Pour qui a vu les ruines du Ghetto
Les faits humains ne sont pas à refaire
Tout doit changer sinon la mort s'installe
Mort est à vaincre ou bien c'est le désert

Or c'est ici que se montre le monstre
Fier de sortir du cœur même de l'homme
De l'homme enchaîné de l'homme rompu
Qui ne voit plus clair qui ne pense plus

Le Ghetto mort son ombre est sous le monstre
Mais son courage fut d'amours communes
D'amours passées qui renaîtront futures
Nouées fleuries de tête et de racines

Have our struggle and our labor failed
Has despair come to sleep in our bed
We dreamed of kissing health and youth
On lips and forehead we still dream of it
Our life will change as a child changes

We have not despaired we still survive
All has been harder darker than ever
But night has not mixed with our blood
One step more together and the pathway bursts
To give us all our well-being and our way.

☉

IN WARSAW
THE FANTASTIC CITY

Whoever has not seen the ruins of the Ghetto
Does not know his body's destiny
When death feasts on it and its heart rots
When its unique absence makes a vacuum

For whoever has seen the ruins of the Ghetto
The human deeds must not be done again
All must change or else death conquers
And death is to be conquered if not we are a
      wilderness

For here the monster shows itself
Proud of springing from the very heart of man
Of man in chains man broken
Who no longer sees clearly who thinks no more

The shadow of the dead Ghetto is beneath the
      monster
But its courage was of mutual loves
Of past loves to be born again as future loves
United flowering in branch and root

213

Et sous le ciel ployant de Varsovie
La longue peine et la souffrance insigne
Défont refont un rêve de bonheur
L'espoir compose un arc-en-ciel de routes

L'homme en terre fait place à l'homme sur la terre.

And beneath the arching sky of Warsaw
Long pain and signal suffering
Undo rebuild a dream of happiness
Hope makes a rainbow of the roads

Man in the earth gives way to man on the earth.

BIBLIOGRAPHY

LE DEVOIR ET L'INQUIETUDE, Editions Gonon, Paris, 1917.

POEMES POUR LA PAIX, (one folded sheet), Paris, July 1918.

LES ANIMAUX ET LEURS HOMMES, LES HOMMES ET LEURS ANIMAUX, Au Sans Pareil, Paris, 1920.

LES NECESSITES DE LA VIE ET LES CONSEQUENCES DES REVES, preceded by EXEMPLES, (preface by Jean Paulhan), Au Sans Pareil, Paris, 1921.

REPETITIONS, (reprinted in *Capitale de la Douleur*), Au Sans Pareil, Paris, 1922.

MOURIR DE NE PAS MOURIR, (reprinted in *Capitale de la Douleur*), NRF, Paris, 1924.

AU DEFAUT DU SILENCE, (principal poems reprinted in *Capitale de la Douleur*), printed without name of author or illustrator, (Max Ernst), 1926.

CAPITALE DE LA DOULEUR, NRF, Paris, 1926.

LE DESSOUS D'UNE VIE, OU LA PYRAMIDE HUMAINE, Les Cahiers du Sud, 1926.

DEFENSE DE SAVOIR, (reprinted in *L'Amour la Poésie*), Editions Surréalistes, Paris 1928.

L'AMOUR LA POESIE, NRF, Paris, 1929.

A TOUTE EPREUVE, (reprinted in *La Vie immédiate*), Editions Surréalistes, Paris, 1930.

DORS, (One folded sheet 20 copies; reprinted in *La Vie Immédiate*), Paris, 1931.

LA VIE IMMEDIATE, Editions des Cahiers Libres, Paris, 1932.

COMME DEUX GOUTTES D'EAU, (reprinted in *La Rose Publique*), Ed. Surréalistes, Paris, 1933.

LA ROSE PUBLIQUE, NRF, Paris, 1934.

NUITS PARTAGEES, (taken from *La Vie Immédiate*, reprinted in *Donner à Voir*), Editions G.L.M., 1935.

FACILE, (reprinted in *Les Yeux Fertiles*), Editions G.L.M., 1935.

LA BARRE D'APPUI, (40 copies), Editions des Cahiers d'Art, Paris, 1936. Reprinted in LES YEUX FERTILES, Editions G.L.M., 1936.

L'EVIDENCE POETIQUE, (reprinted in *Donner à Voir*), Editions G.L.M., 1937.

APPLIQUEE, (24 copies; reprinted in *Donner à Voir*), 1937.

LES MAINS LIBRES, Editions Jeanne Bucher, 1937.

THORNS OF THUNDER, Stanley Nott, Ltd., London, 1937.

QUELQUES-UNS DES MOTS QUI JUSQU'ICI M'ETAIENT MYSTERIEUSEMENT INTERDITS, (reprinted in *Cours Naturel*), Editions G.L.M., 1938.

COURS NATUREL, Editions du Sagittaire, 1938.

MEDIEUSES, (12 copies; reprinted in *Le Livre Ouvert*), 1938.

CHANSON COMPLETE, NRF., Paris, 1939.

DONNER A VOIR, NRF., Paris, 1939.

LE LIVRE OUVERT I (1938-40), Editions des Cahiers d'Art, Paris, 1940, (October).

MORALITE DU SOMMEIL, (reprinted in *Le Livre Ouvert II*), Editions de l'Aiguille Aimantée, Brussels, 1941.

SUR LES PENTES INFERIEURES, (7 poems in the collection *Poètes*, Editions Peau de Chagrin, reprinted in *Le Livre Ouvert II* and *Poésie et Vérité*, 1942), 1941.

CHOIX DE POEMES, 1914-41, NRF, Paris, 1946.

LE LIVRE OUVERT II, 1939-41, Editions des Cahiers d'Art, Paris, 1942, (January), (1947).

LA DERNIERE NUIT, (reprinted in *Poesie et Verite* 1942), 1942.

POESIE INVOLONTAIRE ET POESIE INTENTIONNELLE, Editions *Poésie et Vérité*, Paris, 1942.

POESIE ET VERITE, 1942, Editions de la Main à la Plume, 1942.

POESIE ET VERITE, 1942, (New, enlarged edition), Editions Baconnière, Neûchatel, Switzerland, 1943.

LE LIT LA TABLE, Trois Collines, Geneva, Switzerland, 1944.

LES SEPT POEMES D'AMOUR EN GUERRE, under pseudonym « Jean du Haut », Bibliothèque Française (published clandestinely), 1943.

DIGNES DE VIVRE, Editions Sequana, Paris, 1944.

AU RENDEZ-VOUS ALLEMAND, Editions de Minuit, Paris, 1944.

A PABLO PICASSO, Trois Collines, Geneva, Switzerland, 1945.

POESIE ININTERROMPUE, NRF, Paris, 1946.

A MARC CHAGALL, Editions du Chêne, Paris, 1946.

DOUBLES D'OMBRE, (in collaboration with André Beaudin), NRF, Paris, 1945.

LE DUR DESIR DE DURER, Bordas, 1946. (English version by Stephen Spender, New Directions, 1950.)

PREMIERS POEMES, Editions Mermod, Lausanne, Switzerland, 1948.

POEMES POLITIQUES, Gallimard, Paris, 1948.

VOIR, Trois Collines, Geneva, Switzerland, 1948.

PICASSO A ANTIBES, Drouin, Paris, 1948.

WORKS IN COLLABORATION

with Max Ernst, LES MALHEURS DES IMMORTELS, Librairie Six, Paris, 1922.

with Max Ernst, A L'INTERIEUR DE LA VUE, Editions Seghers, Paris, 1948.

with Benjamin Peret, 152 PROVERBES MIS AU GOUT DU JOUR, Editions Surréalistes, 1925.

with André Breton, L'IMMACULEE CONCEPTION, Editions Surréalistes, Paris, 1930.

NOTES SUR LA POESIE, Editions G.L.M., 1930.

PETIT DICTIONNAIRE ILLUSTRE DU SURREALISME, Editions Beaux-Arts, 1938.

with André Breton and René Char, RALENTIR TRAVAUX, Editions Surréalistes, 1930.

TRANSLATION

with Louis Parrot, ODE A SALVADOR DALI by Federico Garcia Lorca, Editions G.L.M., 1938.

LE MEILLEUR CHOIX DE POEMES, Sagittaire, 1948.

RECORDING

LA VICTOIRE DE GUERNICA, November 1936. Poems read by the author in November 1937.

NOTES

Many poems of Paul Eluard have been set to music by Francis Poulenc, Henri Sauguet, Georges Auric, Edouard Mesens, André Souris, Maurice Jaubert and Robert Caby.

During the Resistance, Eluard wrote under the pseudonyms of Jean du Haut and Maurice Hervent ; in recent years he has used the names Didier Desroches and Brun.

This bibliography was based on one made by Louis Parrot in his critique, Paul Eluard, (Editions Pierre Seghers, Paris, 1945).